VOICES OF A GENERATION

VOICES OF A GENERATION
THREE MILLENNIAL PLAYS

EDITED BY
MICHELLE MACARTHUR

PLAYWRIGHTS CANADA PRESS
TORONTO

First edition: January 2022
Printed and bound in Canada by Imprimerie Gauvin, Gatineau

Jacket art by Pui Yan Fong

Playwrights Canada Press
202-269 Richmond St. W., Toronto, ON M5V 1X1
416.703.0013 | info@playwrightscanada.com | www.playwrightscanada.com

For professional or amateur production rights, please contact Playwrights Canada Press.

LIBRARY AND ARCHIVES CANADA CATALOGUING IN PUBLICATION
Title: Voices of a generation : three millennial plays / edited by Michelle MacArthur.
Other titles: Voices of a generation (MacArthur)
Names: MacArthur, Michelle, editor.
Description: Includes bibliographical references.
Identifiers: Canadiana (print) 20210322608 | Canadiana (ebook) 20210322748
  | ISBN 9780369102966 (softcover) | ISBN 9780369102973 (PDF)
  | ISBN 9780369102980 (HTML)
Subjects: LCSH: Canadian drama—21st century. | CSH: Canadian drama (English)
  —21st century
Classification: LCC PS8315.1 .V65 2021 | DDC c812/.608—dc23

Playwrights Canada Press operates on land which is the ancestral home of the Anishinaabe Nations (Ojibwe / Chippewa, Odawa, Potawatomi, Algonquin, Saulteaux, Nipissing, and Mississauga), the Wendat, and the members of the Haudenosaunee Confederacy (Mohawk, Oneida, Onondaga, Cayuga, Seneca, and Tuscarora), as well as Metis and Inuit peoples. It always was and always will be Indigenous land.

We acknowledge the financial support of the Canada Council for the Arts, the Ontario Arts Council (OAC), Ontario Creates, and the Government of Canada for our publishing activities.

For Simon, my favourite Gen-Xer.

TABLE OF CONTENTS

ACKNOWLEDGEMENTS

My deepest thanks to Annie, Blake, and Jessica at Playwrights Canada Press for supporting this project, which I pitched partially because I wanted an opportunity to work with such a great group of people. The experience did not disappoint! My thanks also to Jess Riley, whose early encouragement and advice helped me to shape my book proposal, and to Karen Fricker, who provided valuable feedback on my introduction. I would also like to express my gratitude to the artists whose works appear in this anthology and to the artists and scholars who contributed introductions to the plays. It has been an honour and a pleasure collaborating with all of you.

My work on this project was supported by the University of Windsor's Humanities Research Group Fellowship in 2019–20, which gave me focused time to dedicate to it and opportunities to share it publicly. One such opportunity was a staged reading of *The Millennial Malcontent*, which I co-directed with my colleague Alice Nelson, whose collaboration I truly appreciate. I want to thank the HRG and its dynamic director, Dr. Kim Nelson, for their enthusiasm for this book and their belief in me.

Several University of Windsor undergraduate students contributed to this book through research assistance and workshop readings: Spencer Allder, Sophie Bouey, Jeremy Burke, Morgan Corbett-Collins, Juli Docherty, Nayantara Ellathur, Celeste Fiallos Castillo, Josh Gregory, Rakesha James, Jonnie Lombard, Avery MacDonald, Julian Macioce, Simone Matheson, Ollie Reid, Olivia Ridpath, Noah Rocha, Kristin Safou, Mehjaas Singh, Safia Suliman, Lauren Watson, Elissa Weir, and Tatyana Wiebe. As a "geriatric" millennial, I am indebted to these younger members of my generation for their generous feedback and for giving me so much hope for the future.

WHO ARE THE VOICES OF A GENERATION?

MICHELLE MACARTHUR

> "I think I might be the voice of my generation. Or, at least, *a* voice
> of *a* generation."
> —Hannah Horvath, *Girls* (Season 1, Episode 1)

Created by and starring Lena Dunham, *Girls* debuted on HBO in 2012 and aired for six seasons, quickly making its mark as what many consider the quintessential millennial television series. In the pilot episode, Dunham's character, Hannah Horvath, is having dinner with her parents, who are visiting her in New York City, when they drop a bomb on her: they are cutting her off. At the end of the episode, Hannah, high from drinking opium tea, shows up at their hotel room and proposes that they pay her a meager $1,100 per month for the next two years so she can finish writing her memoir. In a (losing) bid to convince her parents to keep supporting her, she utters what would become the most notorious line of the series: "I think I might be the voice of my generation. Or, at least, *a* voice of *a* generation." Hannah's famous declaration unleashed lively debate and eye rolling en masse in response to *Girls* and the millennial women it purported to represent. To some, the twentysomething protagonists were entitled, navel-gazing white girls who refused to grow up and acknowledge their privilege; to others, they were a voice of a generation, a generation saddled with student debt and poor job prospects, grappling with the damage done by the generations who had come before.[1]

---

1   For more on the representation of millennial women in *Girls*, see Bell.

The polarized public response to *Girls* is reflective of broader attitudes toward millennials, whose identities have been scrutinized by everyone from demographers to market researchers since the generational group was first labelled three decades ago (Howe and Strauss). While generational lines are variously drawn depending on whom you ask, millennials are generally understood to be the children of the baby boomers and born in the years between the early 1980s and late 1990s.[2] Also known as Generation Y, they are "the first generation to come of age in the new millennium" (Pew Research Center, qtd. in Cairns 7). Communication and cultural studies scholar James Cairns characterizes the time in which millennials came of age as "a period in which the material and emotional burdens of survival have been even more aggressively downloaded onto the individual" (7). This context is significant: as Cairns and many others have pointed out, identifying the exact boundaries that define a generation is less important than understanding the common historical events and experiences that they share (Ng and Johnson 121). For millennials, these markers include the development of the Internet during their formative years, the turn of the twenty-first century, the 2008 economic crisis, and, as Cairns suggests, the entrenchment of neoliberalism. These markers bear many material consequences, such as soaring tuition fees, precarious employment, environmental degradation, and rising costs of living; they also bear emotional consequences, such as the current mental health crisis among millennials (Serpe) and the loneliness and isolation that lurk on the flip side of social networking.

This anthology gathers three Canadian plays to ask what it means to be a millennial. Creative, enterprising, and technologically savvy, millennials have produced a proliferation of images of themselves that complicate demographic analyses and challenge widely held assumptions. These films, television series, digital representations, and, of

---

2   American policy analysts and political consultants Howe and Strauss were the first to use the term "millennial" to describe this generation in 2000, though they had been writing about the demographic earlier in the 1990s; they define the generational boundaries as 1982–1999. Demographer David Foot defines the cohort he also calls baby boom echo as being born between 1980 and 1995; psychologist Jean Twenge marks 1982 as the beginning of the generation.

course, plays, offer complex insights into a much-maligned demographic and deserve serious attention. Within the context of Canadian theatre, while millennials are generating a significant portion of the creative work currently performed on our stages, their plays have yet to be located within broader discourses about their generation. This book contributes to the growing focus on age as an identity category within theatre and performance studies scholarship by considering this often overlooked middle generation. The three plays anthologized here are examples of the diversity of dramatic works by and/or about millennials. By putting them into dialogue with one another and framing each with a critical introduction (two in the case of *Smoke*), this book aims to lay down some generative ideas that might be further developed through a consideration of additional works. Frances Koncan's *zahgidiwin/love* follows Namid through multiple generations: as a survivor of abuse in a residential school in the 1960s, as a missing woman held in a suburban basement in the 1990s, and as the rebellious daughter of a tyrannical queen in a post-apocalyptic, matriarchal society. Described by Koncan as "a decolonial comedy about loss—of language, of love, of culture, of land, of knowledge—in the era of truth and reconciliation," *zahgidiwin/love* examines the lingering effects of intergenerational trauma on Indigenous millennials through a mash-up of theatrical styles and pop cultural intertexts. *The Millennial Malcontent* by Erin Shields is a gender-swapped adaptation of Sir John Vanbrugh's 1697 Restoration Comedy *The Provoked Wife*. It follows a group of young people during a night out for Nuit Blanche in Toronto who, like the characters featured in Vanbrugh's text, chase each other around town, their romantic and sexual pursuits thwarted by the typical conventions of Restoration Comedy such as cross-dressing, mistaken identity, and hiding in closets. Shields's play covers a wide range of millennial themes—from social media stardom and social media addiction, to student debt and post-graduation aimlessness, to social justice and armchair activism, to economic precarity and unemployment—and in its conversation with its source text, asks to what degree the characters' struggles are unique to millennials. Elena Belyea's *Smoke* finds two exes reunited to discuss their conflicting memories of their last night together and the lingering trauma of an assault experienced between them. A two-hander where the role of the accused can be played by a male- or female-identifying actor, it is a nuanced examination of issues and questions surrounding sexual assault and consent that millennials have helped bring to light through their activism and open sharing of their experiences.

The plays in this anthology poke fun at millennial stereotypes while poking holes in them. Even the comic characters in *The Millennial Malcontent*, while on the surface embodying every Gen Y cliché imaginable, incite empathy and understanding as the loneliness underlying their #blessed lives seeps through the cracks of their social media profiles. By highlighting the personal effects of the common historical events that marked Canadian millennials' coming-of-age, these plays question whether millennials really expect too much or whether they are rather grappling with their political, economic, and environmental inheritances and demanding a better future. In so doing, they challenge what Cairns calls the millennial myth of entitlement, which suggests that "young people today, more than at any point in history, take for granted the bounty they've inherited and expect to have praise and a good life handed to them without having to do anything in return" (2). His 2017 book on the same topic aims to debunk this myth, arguing, "To define millennials as the entitled generation isn't just to say that they have high expectations; it's to say that their expectations are too high and that young people ought to settle for less" (14). At the same time, these plays also foreground the impact of factors such as gender, race, and class on individual experiences and the differences they produce within a generation. For example, Koncan's *zahgidiwin/love* exposes the effects of colonialism and patriarchy on Indigenous millennial women, while Belyea's *Smoke* asks its audience to consider how our willingness to believe a survivor of sexual assault is impacted by their identity and ours. In selecting plays that take an intersectional approach to understanding the millennial experience, I want to highlight the value of examining representations of millennials in arts and culture in order to develop a more nuanced picture of the generation than those painted by statistics alone.

Shields, Koncan, and Belyea's plays can, of course, be studied through many other lenses. For example, in her introduction to *The*

Millennial Malcontent, Kailin Wright applies theories of adaptation, feminism, and irony to her discussion of the play. What, then, is the value of studying these plays as millennial plays? I want to suggest that in addition to sharing thematic concerns, these plays are united by common dramaturgical approaches emerging from millennials' tentative relationship to the past, their paradoxical need to both return to the past for comfort and to reject it in order to move forward. This ambivalent nostalgia, as I refer to it, is a product of the historical events that have shaped millennials' diverse experiences as ones marked by transitions. A key example of this is the transition from analogue to digital as millennials came of age. Older millennials like myself can remember a time before cellphones and the Internet, when you had to call your friends on a land line rather than text them and consult hardcover encyclopedias rather than Google for answers to questions. As millennials matured to adulthood, they experienced the rise of the World Wide Web and related technological innovations, which came with promises of freedom, ease, and democracy, but were quickly co-opted by corporate interests that bore profound socio-political and personal costs. Millennials' relationship to this transition remains an ambivalent one: they continually revisit their analogue pasts to seek comfort and pleasure in times of instability, while defining themselves by their use of (and dependence on) digital technologies. This is shown quite explicitly in *The Millennial Malcontent*, as Shields's characters play childhood games like Candy Land and fetishize vinyl records even as they engage in typical Gen-Y, future-directed behaviours, like producing YouTube videos and podcasts.

Millennials' nostalgic urge to return to simpler times is facilitated by unprecedented access to the artefacts of their past through digital tools such as Netflix, iTunes, and other streaming services that enable Gen Y to view movies from their childhood or listen to their favourite 1990s music. At the same time, however, millennials reject the past and the traditions of older generations: there is an urge to reinvent and find new ways forward when the old ways have not worked. This is seen, for example, in what Nick Serpe calls the "youth outrage" that has fuelled social movements like Black Lives Matter, Occupy Wall Street, and #MeToo as well as in millennials' political leanings more broadly. Summarizing recent findings on American millennials from the Pew Research Center, Serpe writes:

> Millennials were more willing than older generations to acknowledge the continuing existence of racism, expressed more positive attitudes about immigrants, were less militaristic and nationalistic, and were more likely to support a "bigger government" that provided health care and welfare. They were more strongly associated with the Democratic Party and more disapproving of Donald Trump than any other generation (younger "post-millennials" were not included in the poll). (9)

While Serpe is careful not to "overstate the extent of millennial leftism," he does suggest that those who "embrace radicalism" are actively finding new ways to undo the damage of previous generations. Serpe's conclusion gestures to millennials' conflicted relationship to the past: "But the millennials who embrace radicalism have turned their shared experiences into a politics that does more than reflect the year they were born. They are less interested in themselves as a discrete category than in their relationships to those who came before and those who will come after" (14).

Ambivalent nostalgia is produced dramaturgically in the plays gathered here in different ways. In *The Millennial Malcontent*, Shields uses adaptation, a form which reaches back to the past for source material, described by Linda Hutcheon as "repetition, but repetition without replication" (7). Yet, as implied in Hutcheon's definition, adaptation creates something entirely new, an independent entity that can be enjoyed on its own with no knowledge of the source text. Hutcheon asserts, "[A]n adaptation is a derivation that is not derivative—a work that is second without being secondary. It is its own palimpsestic thing" (9). Adaptation thus straddles the past and the present, providing, as Wright puts it, "the pleasure of a palimpsest" for those who have experienced both texts. While adaptation has had an enduring appeal for theatre-makers and audiences, it has emerged as a popular form among millennials as a way to push back against the entitlement myth by connecting their experiences with those of previous generations. For example, reviewing Halley Feiffer's *Moscow Moscow Moscow Moscow Moscow Moscow*, an irreverent adaptation that finds Chekhov's three sisters communicating in upspeak and emojis, Alexandra Schwartz writes, "Watching these Russians snipe and complain in our ditzy online-speak gives the lie to the nostalgic fantasy that people were better, kinder, and more 'connected' before our atomized era of screens" (74). Similarly, while Shields's reversal of the characters' gender in her adaptation of *The Provoked Wife* implies a feminist critique of its problematic source text, it also elicits empathy for millennials by highlighting the persistent effects of patriarchy on young people's lives—in both Restoration England and contemporary Canada.

Koncan's *zahgidiwin/love* uses a similar strategy to play with time. As noted earlier, it moves between three different eras, revisiting some of the sources of intergenerational trauma affecting Indigenous millennials today. The play's protagonist, Namid, must journey back through the 1960s and 1990s in order to move forward and restore a matriarchal society in what Koncan, significantly, calls the Retrofuture. But even in these distinct time periods, anachronism abounds. For example, scenes set in the 1960s in Saint Bernadette's Residential School for Wayward Youths with Big Dreams contain references to Jude Law, David Bowie, and Hermione Granger, among others. Koncan thus puts past, present, and future into conversation with one another through both the play's dramaturgical structure and its layering of intertextual references. Media theorist Louisa Stein calls this intertextuality millennial remix culture, which she defines as "the transformative recombination of already existing cultural materials, including reversioned music, mashed-up music, and combinations of video and music" (57). Stein's definition echoes Hutcheon's discussion of adaptation as she asserts that "remix culture is all about audiences becoming authors of culture in their own right" (59). In other words, though remix, like adaptation, is a fraught concept enmeshed in debates about authorship, copyright, and freedom of expression, it is not a parasitic art form. As Koncan reworks source material from the past, she transforms it into something new—in an artistic act of decolonization, she adapts settler-generated cultural material to create what Lindsay Lachance in her introduction names resurgence theatre, "when Indigenous artists work in ways that centre their culturally specific perspectives, experiences, or practices." This aesthetic strategy mirrors Namid's journey within the play. As Lachance notes, rather than showing Indigenous women as oppressed by patriarchal and colonial structures, "Koncan uses the past/present/future to demonstrate how they have always overcome, resisted, and loved their ways out of danger." Fittingly, *zahgidiwin/love* is bookended by Leonard Cohen's "Chelsea Hotel #2" playing from Gitche Manitou's record player, only the first version is Cohen's and the second is millennial artist Lana Del Rey's cover.

Belyea's *Smoke* also moves back and forth between time periods: while the meeting between Jordan and Aiden happens in real time, it is intercut with scenes of each character reading their creative work (poetry and short fiction respectively) in different moments in the future. As Thea Fitz-James argues in her introduction, *Smoke* unfolds within the framework of queer time, which "challenges linear, normative temporalities rooted in heteropatriarchy and capitalism." Queer time, Fitz-James suggests, manifests in the different ways in which Aiden and Jordan have measured the years that have elapsed since they last met and in the dramaturgical structure of the play itself, which weaves together multiple temporalities that affect how the audience experiences the play. By the end of *Smoke*, it is obvious that Jordan and Aiden will never come to an agreement of what transpired between them in their shared past and that in order to move forward, they must cut ties with it—or, as the fire imagery crackling through the play suggests, they must burn it down. The imagery of a controlled burn to make way for regrowth and regeneration finds parallels in the experience of millennial activists, who have a complicated relationship with what came before, on the one hand standing on the shoulders of their forebearers but on the other, paying for the shortcomings of those same forebearers, underlining the need to reject systems of the past and propose radical new solutions. Millennials' participation in the #MeToo movement through sharing accounts of sexual assault on social media bears some resemblance to second-wave feminists' attendance of consciousness raising circles, yet the contemporary movement challenged its predecessors' essentialist view of gender and ignorance of the differences between survivors. As Jenna Rodgers remarks in her introduction, in its attention to social location, *Smoke* asks its audience to reflect on the ways in which identity shapes people's experience of and response to sexual assault. Inspired by the multiple perspectives facilitated by *Smoke*'s dramaturgy and approach to casting, I asked both Fitz-James and Rodgers to write introductions to provide two views on the play.

Taken together, these three plays facilitate—in both form and content—an interrogation of millennials' relationship with past, present, and future and the myths that shape how they are understood. While we would need a much larger sample to make definitive conclusions about how Gen Y is represented in Canadian drama, I offer this collection of three plays as a foundation on which to provoke further conversation. Writing this introduction in early 2021, as Generation Z's mockery of my skinny jeans and side part are trending on social media, I am reminded of the rapid cycle of youth culture and the age-old compulsion to rebel against those who came before.[3] I am also reminded of the need for intergenerational empathy and understanding, which can be achieved much more easily through engagement with creative work like plays than demographic data alone. As we continue to study cultural representations of millennials, it is important to look beyond the most visible examples of this generation and consider the diversity of experiences and identities that constitute it. To return to the example opening this introduction, while many criticisms have been launched against *Girls* for its narrow worldview, as Dunham-as-Horvath suggests in the pilot episode, her voice is *a* voice of a generation, not *the* voice of a generation.

---

3   See, for example, Elan.

WORKS CITED

Bell, Katherine. "'Obvie, We're the Ladies!' Postfeminism, Privilege, and HBO's Newest *Girls*." *Feminist Media Studies*, vol. 13, no. 2, Feb. 2013, pp. 363–66. https://doi.org/10.1080/14680777.2013.771886.

Cairns, James Irvine. *The Myth of the Age of Entitlement: Millennials, Austerity, and Hope*. U of Toronto P, 2017.

Elan, Priya. "'No Skinny Jeans': Gen z Launch TikTok Attack on Millennial Fashion." *The Guardian*, 12 Feb. 2021, https://www.theguardian.com /technology/2021/feb/12/no-skinny-jeans-gen-z-launch-tiktok -attack-millennial-fashion. Accessed 21 Feb. 2021.

Howe, Neil, and William Strauss. *Millennials Rising: The Next Great Generation*. Vintage, 2000.

Hutcheon, Linda. *A Theory of Adaptation*. 2nd ed. Routledge, 2012.

Koncan, Frances. "Truth, Reconciliation, and Zahgidiwin/Love." *Intermission*, 2 May 2016, https://www.intermissionmagazine.ca /artist-perspective/truth-reconciliation-zahgidiwinlove/. Accessed 2 Feb. 2021.

Ng, Eddy s.w., and Jasmine McGinnis Johnson. "Millennials: Who Are They, How Are They Different, and Why Should We Care?" *The Multi-Generational and Aging Workforce: Challenges and Opportunities*, edited by Ronald J. Burke, Cary L. Cooper, and Alexander-Stamatios G. Antoniou, Elgar, 2015, pp. 121–37.

Norris, Doug. "Millennials: The Newest, Biggest, and Most Diverse Target Market." Environics Analytics 9th Annual User Conference, Nov. 2015, Toronto. http://www.environicsanalytics.ca/docs /default-source/eauc2015-presentations/dougnorris-afternoonplenary. pdf?sfvrsn=6%20. Accessed 10 Oct. 2017.

"Pilot." *Girls*, created by Lena Dunham, season 1, episode 1, HBO, 15 Apr. 2012. *Crave*, https://www.crave.ca/en/tvshows/girls.

Schwartz, Alexandra. "A Millennial Reboot of Chekhov, and 'Moulin Rouge' on Broadway." *New Yorker*, 5 and 12 Aug. 2019, https://www.newyorker.com/magazine/2019/08/05/a-millennial-reboot-of-chekhov-and-moulin-rouge-on-broadway. Accessed 25 Feb. 2021.

Serpe, Nick. "Beyond Generational Politics: Do Millennials Constitute a Political Category?" *New Labor Forum*, vol. 28, no. 2, 2019, pp. 8–15. https://doi.org/10.1177/1095796019838835.

Stein, Louisa Ellen. *Millennial Fandom: Television Audiences in the Transmedia Age*. U of Iowa P, 2015.

ZAHGIDIWIN/LOVE

FRANCES KONCAN

BUILDING A DAM OF ANISHINAABEG LOVE: RESURGENCE IN FRANCES KONCAN'S *ZAHGIDIWIN/LOVE*

LINDSAY LACHANCE

A few weeks ago I received a text message from Frances, telling me that she had seen a beaver (amik) in the river while walking her dog. There are only approximately a hundred beavers living in the Red River in the city of Winnipeg, so this ancestral visit was meaningful. Frances described how amik was busy working, chewing, and then carrying a tree branch up river, showing its strength, beauty, and resilience.

For urban Anishinaabeg women, there is much joy in seeing our ancestors out and about in city centres. Michi Saagiig Nishnaabeg scholar, writer, and artist Leanne Betasamosake Simpson shares four stories that offer teachings about amik in her 2020 Kreisel Lecture, entitled "A Short History of the Blockade: Giant Beavers, Diplomacy, and Regeneration in Nishnaabewin." Simpson links amik and its dam building to the resilience seen in Indigenous youth building blockades and attending protests. Amik's industriousness, intelligence, care, and love needed to sustain good relationships with the earth is mirrored in the actions of those participating in the Idle No More movement, the Dakota Access Pipeline protests, the Wet'suwet'en resistances, or the Murdered and Missing Indigenous Women and Girls marches. Amik's dam builds community for the beaver family and demonstrates ethics of care and love in its construction process.

Frances Koncan's *zahgidiwin/love* is also a dam made of industriousness, intelligence, care, and love. It is a structure of Anishinaabeg brilliance that is built to overcome the flood. *zahgidiwin/love* follows an

Indigenous woman called Namid through a past, present, and retrofuture saturated with colonial patriarchal violence. Journeying through a residential school, a suburban basement, and a crumbling palace, Namid finds strength in her lineage and culture that frees her from these oppressive forces. In this introduction, I discuss *zahgidiwin/love* through a resurgence framework. Looking to the Seven Anishinaabeg Teachings and Jill Carter's (Anishinaabe) use of "soft power," I discuss the play's themes of language, gender, and intergenerational relationships to show how it illustrates the principles of Indigenous resurgence theatre.

BUILDING THE DAM: UNDERSTANDING RESURGENCE

Resurgence theories are still very much rooted in political theory and do not look to artistic practice as much as they should. Resurgence means many things to different Indigenous scholars and artists, and Indigenous resurgence theatre will take on various forms depending on the artists involved and the stories being shared. For me, Indigenous resurgence theatre is when Indigenous artists work in ways that centre their culturally specific perspectives, experiences, or practices. For Simpson, resurgence is "dancing on our turtle's back; it is visioning and dancing new realities and worlds into existence" (*Dancing* 70). This definition is very similar to the responsibility of the playwright: someone who creates worlds with specific rules, geographies, tone, and purpose.

Within *zahgidiwin/love*, Koncan provides various locations across Turtle Island that highlight and care for Indigenous historical, present, and potentially future experiences. Turtle Island is used by many Indigenous and non-Indigenous folks to refer to North America, without having to recognize enforced colonial boarders. Skywoman falling through the sky and landing on a turtle's back is also a part of many nations' (including Anishinaabe, Haudenosaunee, and Cree) creation stories. Expanding her notion of resurgence described above, Simpson writes in her book, *Dancing on Our Turtle's Back*, that after Skywoman landed on the turtle's back and muskrat brought up some dirt from the extreme depths of the water, she spread the earth on the shell with her feet and danced creation into being.[1] Presencing[2] Turtle Island in this piece honours the echoes of Skywoman's creation story and facilitates jumps in time and space. As the play moves between temporalities and geographies, *zahgidiwin/love* questions if the story at its centre is a new one being told for the first time or if Namid's experiences are actually the residue of her Indigenous ancestors' and kin's actions. Koncan creates these intersecting locations and times to demonstrate the ongoing and contemporary ways that patriarchal and colonial structures enact physical and symbolic violence on Indigenous women. However, instead of showing Indigenous women oppressed by these systems, Koncan uses the past/present/future to demonstrate how these women have always overcome, resisted, and loved their way out of danger. As Koncan repeats in the limbos of the prologue and the epilogue, we move from darkness, to light, to certainty.

zahgidiwin/love has Anishinaabemowin (the Anishinaabe language) in the title itself, signalling that language carries importance in this piece. Since resurgence theories involve self-reflective work that looks to the past to radically transform the future, the use of Anishinaabemowin throughout the text plays a significant role in reclaiming and centring Anishinaabeg intelligences. Gitche Manitou's Record Player, meaning the Great Spirit's Record Player, is a named character who bookends the piece by first playing Leonard Cohen's "Chelsea Hotel #2" and then finishing with Lana Del Rey's cover of the same song, demonstrating, perhaps, a feminine shift in Gitche Manitou itself and showing an awakening of Indigenous feminine power from both the living and the spirit worlds. Powerfully, language is both used intermittently and silenced throughout the piece. Father Aloysius and Sister Agnes forbid the speaking of Anishinaabemowin in the residential school and the Queen reacts violently to it being spoken in her palace several decades later. Although the Queen demonstrates fear and anger when her traditional language is spoken, Namid, her daughter and one who represents a younger generation, is proud

---

1 See chapter four of *Dancing on Our Turtle's Back* for the sharing of the story.

2 Presencing is a way to articulate self-recognition in action, and a term I discuss in greater depth in my dissertation. See Lachance.

and longs to speak it. As the dam within Namid grows stronger, she remembers and speaks her traditional name, inciting a huge act of colonial refusal and cultural resurgence.

STRUCTURING A WORLD THROUGH ANISHINAABEG VALUES: THE SEVEN GRANDFATHER TEACHINGS

The development process of *zahgidiwin/love*, like the content and style of the play itself, also embodies the values of Indigenous resurgence theatre through its rooting in the Seven Grandfather Teachings. As a dramaturg, I use the Seven Grandfather Teachings to refuse working within the well-made-play structure, and to highlight Anishinaabeg theory and worldview. Although versions of the values vary slightly in spelling and in words themselves (for example, some people use Bravery and some use Courage), I have been taught that the Seven Teachings were given to the Anishinaabeg to help guide us toward living a good life. Simpson writes the teachings as "Aakde'ewin, the art of having courage; Debwewin, the art of truth or sincerity; Mnaadendiwin, the art of having respect; Gwekwaadiziwin, the art of being honest; Nbwaakawin, the art of wisdom; Ddadendiziwin, the art of humility; and Zaagidewin, the art of love or loving" (*Dancing* 124–25). In embodying and practising the seven values of Love, Respect, Humility, Courage, Truth, Honesty, and Wisdom, we strive to be our best selves in acknowledging and honouring all of creation under these principles. Being grounded in Anishinaabeg values and ethics in our everyday lives is important. So why not carry these values into our artistic practices as well?

I have had the honour of working as Frances's dramaturg on both *zahgidiwin/love*[3] and *Women of the Fur Trade*. When collaborating as two Anishinaabeg theatre artists, it came naturally to work within the framework of the Seven Grandfather Teachings, presencing them throughout the dramaturgical and rehearsal processes. As the dramaturg, I centre the values in our conversations with actors, asking questions like,

---

3   Lindsay Lachance was *zahgidiwin/love*'s dramaturg during its development phase at Native Earth Performing Arts's 2015 Weesageechak Begins to Dance Festival.

"Which value is your character carrying in this moment? How does that affect the overall world of the play?" We also use the teachings to model how to treat ourselves, and our collaborators—the values get posted on the studio walls as reminders of how to be in relationship with each other. Centring the art of love or loving in the title of the piece is an example of honouring the teachings and centring soft power.

MAPPING RESURGENCE THROUGH SOFT POWER

Jill Carter's essay "Sovereign Proclamations of the Twenty-First Century: Scripting Survivance Through the Language of Soft Power" is particularly useful when considering Indigenous dramaturgies as moments of resurgence and labours of love. Carter explores how performing the Indigenous self is a sovereign act of resistance to the hard powers of settler colonialism. She emphasizes that by using soft power (nurturing, loving, standing firm in personal beliefs), Indigenous peoples are finding artistic sovereignty within the theatrical process. In *zahgidiwin/love*, Koncan offers many opportunities to discuss discrimination toward Indigenous women. Namid and Missing Girl #24601, while being captured by the Heterosexual White Male (HWM), transform from "holding their breath for a lifetime" to taking action, which brings on the great flood. They demonstrate their soft power when they gently and satirically refuse to be HWM's captives. As they summon the flood, they remind him that everything under the moon is Indigenous and belongs to all of creation, not to him alone. They tell him he must die so that they can live. The women in this piece demonstrate the importance of love, caring for others, building community, and discovering/loving self as sovereign acts of resurgence. Namid learns to forgive her mother who is carrying residential school trauma, and learns to love herself in remembering her traditional name.

In her essay, Carter reminds readers that love means many things including caring for the land, honouring Elders, and "asserting Indigenous voice and agency within a dominant society governed by patriarchal powers" (49). This articulation of sovereignty as a process of love is useful when considering *zahgidiwin/love* to be its own version of a beaver's dam. *zahgidiwin/love*, like amik's dam, creates a space that discusses gender discrimination, intergenerational trauma and healing, youth resisting violent home lives, and the struggle of preserving Indigenous languages in an abstracted way that makes readers feel cared for and supported. Like amik building her dam to visit with other beavers, to share stories, and to keep warm, Koncan gently, satirically, and intelligently centres resilient Indigenous women. They set up peaceful protests and stand behind their blockades of self and familial love and resist a history that does not tell their story. And after the flood, they will jump back in the river, and start building more dams.

WORKS CITED

Carter, Jill. "Sovereign Proclamations of the Twenty-First Century: Scripting Survivance Through the Language of Soft Power." *Performing Indigeneity*, edited by Yvette Nolan and Ric Knowles, Playwrights Canada, 2016, pp. 33–65. New Essays on Canadian Theatre 6.

Lachance, Lindsay. *The Embodied Politics of Relational Indigenous Dramaturgies*. 2018. U of British Columbia, PH.D. dissertation. https://open.library.ubc.ca/media/stream/pdf/24/1.0363947/4. Accessed 29 Oct. 2021.

Simpson, Leanne Betasamosake. "2020 CLC Kreisel Lecture with Leanne Betasamosake Simpson | A Short History of the Blockade." *YouTube*, 12 Jun. 2020, https://www.youtube.com/watch?v=8Jb-p7uzj_YM. Accessed 29 Oct. 2021.

———. "The Brilliance of the Beaver: Learning from an Anishnaabe World." *Ideas*, 16 Apr. 2020, https://www.cbc.ca/radio/ideas/the-brilliance-of-the-beaver-learning-from-an-anishnaabe-world-1.5534706. Accessed 29 Oct. 2021.

———. *Dancing on Our Turtle's Back*. Arbeiter Ring, 2011.

zahgidiwin/love premiered at the 2016 Winnipeg Fringe Festival with the following cast and creative team:

Namid: Kelsey Wavey
Sister Agnes / Missing Girl #24601 (MG2) / The Duchess: Bev Katherine
Father Aloysius / Heterosexual White Male (HWM) / The Queen: Erin Meagan Schwartz
Men / Furniture: Aaron Pridham
Men / Furniture: Jonathan Mourant
Men / Furniture: Andrew Vineberg

Stage Manager: Angelica Schwartz
Director and Designer: Frances Koncan

PEOPLE

Actor 1: Namid
Actor 2: Sister Agnes, Missing Girl #24601 (MG2), The Duchess
Actor 3: Father Aloysius, Heterosexual White Male (HWM), The Queen
Actor 4 (optional): Accoutrements
Actor 5 (optional): Furnishings
Actor 6 (live or voice recording): Narrator, Judeo-Christian Overlords, Gitche Manitou's Record Player, the Speaker of the House of the Pagan Gods

PLACES

Turtle Island
The Prologue: limbo
The Past: a residential school, the 1960s
The Present: a suburban basement, the 1990s
The Retrofuture: a crumbling palace, the 2030s
The Epilogue: limbo

1

NARRATOR: Prologue. Limbo. An empty stage. Darkness.

Darkness.

Out of the darkness there is light. *(whispered)* Light.

Light.

Out of the light there is certainty. Certainty?

Certainty.

Out of that certainty is a man.

HETEROSEXUAL WHITE MALE (HWM) enters.

He stands centre stage, right where he belongs.

He stands centre stage.

He waves.

He waves.

Out of that man's rib are two women.

Enter NAMID and MISSING GIRL #24601 (MG2).

They are as of yet uncertain . . . but will ultimately prevail. They step forward. Their footsteps are heavy with the weight of a history that does not tell their story.

    HWM sits.

Meanwhile, the Man sits in his comfortable chair. He will do this for the rest of his life. His ill-fitting jeans are dirty and worn, and his shirt has pizza stains on it. Still, he knows he's a catch.

    Leonard Cohen's "Chelsea Hotel #2" begins to play on GITCHE
    MANITOU'S RECORD PLAYER. NARRATOR's *lines that follow are*
    interspersed between verses, with the final line of the song play-
    ing immediately before NARRATOR's *last line.*

The women stare straight ahead and wait.

The man leans back in his chair and takes up space, saluting a grand tradition.

The women fix their hair and makeup.

They become objects of great value.

The man claps and groans, like a dude-bro lifting weights too heavy for him at the gym.

The women hold their breath for as long as they can.

    The women inhale.

If possible, a lifetime.

    The women hold their breath.

2

NARRATOR: The Retrofuture, Chapter One. A bedroom in an ancient castle in the post-colonial, post-apocalyptic future.

THE SPEAKER OF THE HOUSE OF THE PAGAN GODS: Deep in the Forest of Equality, within castle walls that once crumbled under the weight of the patriarchy but are now rebuilt on the foundations of truthiness and reconciliation, upon a mountaintop so high that even the clouds can't rain on its parade, sits a perfect family, a happy family . . .

Enter NAMID.

. . . a family whose matriarchal rule has spread peace and joy across the land, and whose most beautimous Queen and her deeply ungrateful daughter—

NAMID: Excuse me?

THE SPEAKER OF THE HOUSE OF THE PAGAN GODS: —are today preparing for a very special occasion. While our most benevolent, democratic Queen is as timeless and ageless as a vampire in a young adult novel, today her burden of a daughter celebrates her sixteenth birthday.

Beat.

NAMID: Is that everything? Are you finished?

Beat.

THE SPEAKER OF THE HOUSE OF THE PAGAN GODS: Yep

NAMID *addresses the audience directly.*

NAMID: The Speaker of the House of the Pagan Gods has a tongue of snakes and lies. That is all propaganda.

THE QUEEN enters, followed by FURNISHINGS and ACCOUTREMENTS.

My mother, the Queen, always wears a black dress. It is very long and made of the finest velvet. When she walks—which she has been known to do, when "the moment is right"—it makes a swishing, swooshing, shuffling sound, like this:

THE QUEEN begins to walk in a circle, surveying her kingdom.

Swish swoosh, swish swoosh, swish swoosh, swish swoosh, swish swoosh, swish swoosh, and so on and so forth for as long as she moves until the end of time arrives and she comes to a complete stop.

THE QUEEN stops walking.

Upon her feet, which are actually hooves—but nobody knows so please don't tell—are big black combat boots. They are polished every day, because—

THE QUEEN: It is important to take care of things, and blood is such an unpleasant sight for the peasants and their families.

NAMID: The boots themselves are ominous little creatures. Their heavy footfalls drill in to your ears and turn anyone who hears them to stone. There is nowhere to hide from them, and even if you could . . . well, there won't be anywhere else to go once the flood arrives.

THE QUEEN: I got these in Vietnam, when I was fighting in the war. I was on this boat in the deepest jungle when it suddenly capsized. Everyone else on the boat drowned, and I alone survived. That's called natural selection. I chopped down trees and befriended a tiger and made a raft and floated down the river for weeks all alone, with nothing but the glow of my red lipstick to light my way. The horror! The horror! When I eventually encountered humanity once again, the men of the group were so overcome by my beauty and my kindness that they bestowed upon me these boots and crowned me as their Queen, and that is how I met your father—may he rest in peace—and now here I am, ruler and rightful owner of this great land, this land that is our birthright, this land that was stolen from us so many years ago, Queen and Mother and Saint and Hero, beloved by all who encounter me, and universally admired for my humility and my modesty.

She smiles at no one in particular. A long pause.

NAMID: Okaaaay.

Beat.

I mean, that sounds fake, but okay.

THE QUEEN coughs.

3

NARRATOR: The Past, Chapter One. A classroom in a residential school in the not-distant-enough past.

FATHER ALOYSIUS and SISTER AGNES are doing vocal warm-ups while NAMID sits in a chair in a classroom of one, the loneliest number.

JUDEO-CHRISTIAN OVERLORDS: Saint Bernadette's Residential School for Wayward Youths with Big Dreams. Here in a rickety wood building on the rockity shores of a rainity lake live and work the vessels of the Lord. Behold these most holiest of holy figures as they go about their heavenly business. Bear witness to their eternal glory as they systematically destroy an entire culture.

SISTER AGNES: Requiem aternum dominae! My name is Sister Agnes and I'm here to teach you about the Lord and Saviour Jesus Christ and all he has done to save your heathen soul from eternal damnation.

FATHER ALOYSIUS: And I am Father Aloysius, lead priest in the Lord's Band of Holiness, burdened with glorious purpose to assimilate your savageness and lead it righteously to the path of civilization! Blessed are those who rock out to the electric guitar of Jesus Christ and his band of merry men, who stole from the rich and gave to the poor so that we might enter in to the gates of heaven!

    NAMID raises her hand.

SISTER AGNES: Yes, child?

NAMID: That's Robin Hood.

FATHER ALOYSIUS: Nonsense.

SISTER AGNES: Nonsense!

NAMID: Jesus didn't have merry men. He had apostles.

FATHER ALOYSIUS: Nonsense.

SISTER AGNES: Nonsense! Jesus had disciples, dear.

FATHER ALOYSIUS: Matthew, Mark, Luke, and/or John.

NAMID: Those are the evangelists.

FATHER ALOYSIUS: Non—

SISTER AGNES: —sense! You know not of what you speak. You are young and new to the ways of the Lord.

NAMID: I'm almost sixteen years old. I've been at this stupid school for almost a decade. You stole me from my mother's arms and told her I was going to become a famous rock star, but I haven't. The band isn't getting better. We never even practise.

FATHER ALOYSIUS: I agree, we don't seem to value arts education at this school as much as we should.

SISTER AGNES: Nonsense, Father. Let's stick to the important subject at hand, shall we? If those are the so-called evangelists, then who are Thaddeus—

FATHER ALOYSIUS: Andrew?

SISTER AGNES: Matthew?

FATHER ALOYSIUS: John?

SISTER AGNES: Philip?

FATHER ALOYSIUS: Bartholomew?

SISTER AGNES: Simon?

FATHER ALOYSIUS: Other Simon?

SISTER AGNES: James?

FATHER ALOYSIUS: Other James?

SISTER AGNES: Thomas?

FATHER ALOYSIUS: And that last one. What's his name again? The handsome Black fellow in the excellent jumpsuit? Great singing voice, super loyal? I always forget. Judan? Judat? Jumanji? Jude Law?

NAMID: . . . Judas?

FATHER ALOYSIUS: Ah, yes. Him.

NAMID: Those are the apostles. Oh.

FATHER ALOYSIUS: Oh.

SISTER AGNES: Oh!

FATHER ALOYSIUS: Hmm.

SISTER AGNES: Hmm!

FATHER ALOYSIUS: We have truly taught you well.

SISTER AGNES: Truly, taught you well, we have!

FATHER ALOYSIUS: This school exists to foster the autonomy of your people through successful industrialization, and you are well on your way.
Mazel tov!

> *FATHER ALOYSIUS gives NAMID and SISTER AGNES a high-five. Together they laugh and smile, until FATHER ALOYSIUS has a sudden change of heart.*

Your body is a temple of sin.

> *He sneezes.*

4

NARRATOR: The Present, Chapter One. A suburban basement in the 1990s.

A toilet flushes. HWM enters.

A Heterosexual White Male enters. He sits and rubs his belly like it's a fat, furry cat.

NAMID and MG2 enter and stand behind him.

HWM: Come, my most useful possessions, and join me for dinner. I have prepared a great feast.

NAMID opens her mouth to speak but is silenced.

MG2: Shh. Don't. It's not the right time. Wait until the flood comes.

NAMID: But he did not prepare the feast.

MG2: Shh! Sure he did! See, it's all right here. Mmm, feast.

(to HWM) Such a delicious feast made by a most magnanimous man!

NAMID: We prepared a feast. We: me and you, you and I. And I want credit for my work and equal pay.

MG2: But the flood will come soon and balance will be restored. Does it do any harm if we just let him take credit until then?

NAMID: We can't just wait for a flood to deus-ex-machina us out of captivity and back to our homes and families.

MG2: I don't think it's a deus ex machina if we're relying on it from the beginning.

NAMID: I don't think it's a deus ex machina if it isn't even real!

MG2: It *is* real. When the Supreme Queen's ungrateful daughter turns sixteen years old and enslaves her first man, the deluge will begin and all oppression will be washed away.

NAMID: Dumb. Water doesn't wash away the past. There can be no healing until our oppressors acknowledge their crimes against my ancestors and—

MG2: You know that sort of talk makes me uncomfortable. Anyway, white people have it just as bad! Now, can we please eat? I want cake.

NAMID: Vanilla cake?

MG2: Rude.

HWM clears his throat.

HWM: I have asked you both to join me here tonight for this great feast I have prepared with my own two capable hands, which are very big, and you know what they say about men with big hands, aha-ha-ha, ahe-he-he, haw-haw-haw . . .

NARRATOR: The man leans back in his chair and spreads his legs far apart, making sure everyone notices that he has a penis in there somewhere.

He slaps NAMID on the butt.

NAMID: Enough!

HWM screams.

MG2: Oh my goodness, are you okay?

He screams again and falls out of his chair.

NARRATOR: Up until this exact moment, the man has not heard a single word they have said. In fact, he has been unaware up until now that women are even capable of speaking, and I'm afraid the news comes as a great shock to him.

HWM: You can talk?!

NAMID: Of course we can talk.

MG2: Are you okay? Did you hurt yourself? Can I get you some tea?

HWM: I cannot believe I own not one talking woman but two. Two! Oh me, oh my, my goodness, my gracious, isn't this just the wow, wow, gosh, wow, gosh wow gosh! That is special. I've never kidnapped a woman who could talk before. Are there more of your kind?

NAMID: A few.

HWM: Holy moly. Shucks. Well. Help me up.

NARRATOR: The man extends both hands into the air and squirms helplessly on the floor like a useless baby.

MG2 tries to grabs his hand, but NAMID slaps it away.

NAMID: First, say please.

HWM: Help me up.

NAMID: Say please!

HWM: Help me up!

NAMID: Saaay. Puuuuhleaze.

HWM: I said heeeeeeelllllllllp meup.

NAMID: And I said you have to say please.

HWM: P . . . p . . . p . . . p . . . lice? Puh-loice. Puh-layce. Puh-leeee . . . aaaa . . . seeeaah.

> NAMID *extends her hand and the man takes it. She pulls him halfway up.*

NAMID: Why did you kidnap us?

HWM: Dunno. You seemed like an easy target.

MG2: What about me? My family will be looking for me!

HWM: Truuuue, but you're not blond. I'd be more worried if you were blond.

> NAMID *drops him back to the ground, hard.*

Ow.

NAMID: Getting real sick of your shit.

> MG2 *helps* HWM *back into his chair.*

Great. That's just great, Patty Hearst.

MG2: Being kidnapped is no excuse for bad manners.

HWM: Agreed. Truly, I have taught you well. Now, won't you poh-lease both join me for dinner. I have prepared a great feast.

5

THE SPEAKER OF THE HOUSE OF THE PAGAN GODS: We return now to the heroine of all stories, our eternal leader of this completely equal utopia, the kindliest, goodliest, least superficial Queen.

THE QUEEN: What the hell are you wearing?

NAMID: It's called rezpunk, Mother, and I invented it.

THE QUEEN: Are you trying to make me puke? You'll never enslave men of your own at this rate.

NAMID: I don't want to enslave any men. I'm anti-slavery.

THE QUEEN: Well, you can't freeload in my castle forever. Someday you will have to move out, and you'll need furniture of your own.

NAMID: I don't want furniture.

(with great emotion) I just want to be free!

(to audience) My mother's corset is made of whalebone. It is laced so tight that she can barely breathe. In lieu of breathing, she prefers to devour people whole, which is good for the skin but gives her a stomach ache.

A bell rings.

THE QUEEN: Ugh, family.

Enter THE DUCHESS, looking fab.

Hello, sister.

THE DUCHESS: Hey, bitch. Where's the coke?

NAMID: (*to audience*) She means cake.

THE DUCHESS: Mmm. Cake. Don't you guys just love cake? I just love it. Chocolate, vanilla, red velvet, ice cream cake, birthday cake, wedding cake, funeral cake, cupcakes, tiramisu—is that a kind of cake? Yum!—fruitcake, angel food cake, pound cake, pancakes, even pies, I even like pies, guys, apple pies, cherry pie, pumpkin pie—ow!

    THE QUEEN slaps THE DUCHESS.

THE QUEEN: You need to stop.

THE DUCHESS: Sorry.

(*to NAMID*) So, are you excited for the ceremony? What kind of man are you looking for, specifically? I like my men like I like my cake.

NAMID: You gonna elaborate on that?

THE DUCHESS: Naw.

NAMID: I'm not looking for a man.

THE DUCHESS: But where will you sit?

NAMID: On the floor, I guess. Or maybe I'll stand.

THE DUCHESS: I understand your reservations, but, you know, the natural strength of a man is an evolutionary tactic that makes them better at being furniture. They were meant to do this work.

NAMID: When I am Queen, I will make this kingdom a place of real equality, where no person will ever have to do anything they don't want to do.

THE QUEEN: You're going to give me a heart attack.

NAMID: I dare not hope for such a wonderful gift! I am not that lucky!

THE QUEEN: Off with her head!

THE QUEEN stands. FURNISHINGS prepares for a beheading.

NAMID: Mother! You are such an embarrassment!

THE DUCHESS: I can see her point. Sometimes I wonder if maybe I shouldn't have let you enslave my husband to be your chair.

(to FURNISHINGS) Hey, babe.

FURNISHINGS waves.

THE QUEEN: Off with both their heads!

ACCOUTREMENTS prepares for a second beheading.

THE DUCHESS: They already did that to me! Be more original.

THE QUEEN: How dare either of you speak ill of this kingdom and of its ruler. This world in which you freeload is nothing if not a free and equal land of the most idyllic democracy.

THE DUCHESS: In my kingdom, we—

THE QUEEN: Your kingdom is a colonial, patriarchal wasteland.

THE DUCHESS: And yours is a dictatorship! You couldn't keep a man so you had to enslave them instead!

THE QUEEN: Beheading is too kind. Crucify her!

NAMID: Mother! You can't just crucify people in a democracy.

Beat.

You have to vote on it first.

THE QUEEN: All in favour of the crucifixion of my sister, raise your hand now or suffer the torturous consequences.

> *Everybody except THE DUCHESS raises their hand, in varying levels of reluctance and petulance. THE DUCHESS cries. Her wails are loud and high-pitched.*

Vomit. Could you put a stop to this disgusting display of humanity before I am forced to do something I will regret?

NAMID: (*to audience*) My mother loves watching public executions but has little patience for displays of human emotion.

THE QUEEN: Joan, did you not hear my request? Joan! Joan, h-why are you being so impotent?

NAMID: (*to audience*) She means insolent.

THE QUEEN: Joan, I ask you to do this one thing for me, this one simple thing, for me, your mother, the person who gave you life. I have given you so much, Joan, and you are so ungrateful. You are so unworthy of my love, Joan. Why are you such a disappointment, Joan? Joan, why are you such a failure? Why will you never amount to anything, Joan? Why was I cursed with a—

NAMID: Maybe because my name isn't Joan!!!!

> *THE DUCHESS stops crying.*

THE QUEEN: What? Are you sure?

NAMID: Yes.

THE QUEEN: How sure?

NAMID: Like, pretty sure.

THE QUEEN: So, you're not Joan? Hmm. Maybe Joan is one of my other, better daughters.

NAMID: (*to audience*) My mother has no other children. She only has me, and an increasingly high capacity for self-delusion.

THE QUEEN: So, what is your name then?

NAMID looks confused. THE DUCHESS sniffles.

NAMID: It's . . . it's . . . I can't remember.

NAMID inhales.

6

FATHER ALOYSIUS tunes his guitar while SISTER AGNES sings the blues. NAMID is practising her scales on the piano.

SISTER AGNES: The piano is the most civilized of all the instruments.

FATHER ALOYSIUS: Shut up. Can't you see I'm working on a new hook?

SISTER AGNES: You're right, Father. This is no time for foolish games. We are in the middle of an assimilation.

NAMID: Assimilation? I thought I was here to be in the band and learn autonomy through industrialization.

SISTER AGNES: Enough. Have you finished practising your scales, child?

NAMID: Yeah, I guess, but—

SISTER AGNES: Then let's begin.

NAMID: Begin what?

FATHER ALOYSIUS: You have wandered lonely as a cloud in the bush for far too long. We have generously taken you in and given you a shot at fame, fortune, and eternal life. Are you ready to devote your life to the Lord?

NAMID: Maybe? Will I get to see my family again? I miss them.

SISTER AGNES: No. Your family forced you to play an integral part in your community, while we offer you a comfortable life of ease where you won't have to worry about things like making decisions or the economy.

NAMID: Will I have to give up my language? My traditions?

FATHER ALOYSIUS: Yes. You must drink this metaphor blood and eat this metaphor body and learn to speak English and turn and face the strange ch-ch-changes!

NAMID: But what about my home? The land? My ancestors?

SISTER AGNES: Your people find balance in the resources of the natural world . . . but we offer you mass exploitation that will benefit you enormously in the short term.

FATHER ALOYSIUS: In our world, your youth will be celebrated and respected.

NAMID: And when I am an elder? Will I be respected then?

SISTER AGNES: Best just enjoy life while you're young, dear.

FATHER ALOYSIUS: Our hard-partying, rock-and-or-roll lifestyle can't last forever. Today you become a man. L'chaim.

He makes an invisible toast, and together the three drink an invisible drink.

Now.

SISTER AGNES: Now. Remind us . . . what is your name, child?

NAMID: . . . I don't remember.

FATHER ALOYSIUS: Good.

SISTER AGNES: Gooood.

NAMID: Why don't I remember?

SISTER AGNES: It is His plan. It was He who brought you here.

FATHER ALOYSIUS: Here, where we rock and roll all night—

SISTER AGNES: Carpe noctum.

FATHER ALOYSIUS: And party every day.

SISTER AGNES: Carpe diem. You must have a new name, child.

FATHER ALOYSIUS: By the power vested in me, by the Grace of God, with the magic of my wand, I hereby doth declare you forevermore to be Mary—

SISTER AGNES: Oh, please not Mary, we have so many Marys.

FATHER ALOYSIUS: You shall henceforth be known as . . . Joan?

SISTER AGNES: Joan, after the most venerable Saint Joan, who led the French to freedom and to cake.

NAMID: Thank you both for this precious gift.

FATHER ALOYSIUS: Amen! It will serve you well when the deluge is upon us. Welcome to your new life, Joan. Welcome and beware.

Hallelujah.

SISTER AGNES: Wingardium leviosa.

SISTER AGNES chops off NAMID's hair.

7

NARRATOR: Monday. The Man sits with entitlement upon his three-chair throne. He sips and slurps his food like Jabba the Hutt, and it must be very delicious indeed for it all dribbles out the side of his mouth and down his big, hairy pot-belly that he rubs and rubs in circles like he's sham-wowing a car on a late-night television infomercial.

HWM eats and eats and eats and eats. There is a distant rumble of thunder.

MG2: Sounds like rain.

NAMID: Yeah . . . it does.

They share a conspiratorial look, as NAMID wonders if perhaps the flood is not a myth after all.

HWM: Ya know, I've been doing a lot of thinking. While I'm thrilled to own two talking women, I have got to admit that I'm a little worried. You two just talk way too much and seem to completely dominate the conversation. I can barely get a word in!

He eats and eats and eats and eats.

I've noticed that you ladies are not eating. Is the food I cooked for you okay?

NAMID: The food *we* cooked is great.

MG2: She . . . (*looks at* NAMID) I mean we are just a little upset.

HWM: Women always are.

NAMID: We cannot break bread with you.

HWM: Is it that time of the month?

MG2: We are worried about the flood.

HWM: Women always are. Is it that time of the year?

NAMID: You're an asshole and liar.

MG2: What she means is, sometimes it's frustrating that you take credit for the things that we do.

HWM: What? Like what?

NAMID: Like everything!

MG2: Like the feast we cooked and *you* took credit for.

HWM: Don't be ridiculous. That's just semitics, and I hate semitics! I'm anti-Semitic!

MG2 gasps.

NAMID: He means semantics.

MG2: But semantics are all we have.

HWM: Huh. I understand. You have prepared a great feast. You have been domesticated by me and have prepared a great feast. And since I own you, I own this feast, and therefore it could be argued that I have in fact prepared it. Now, uh, you. What's your name again?

NAMID: You know I don't remember!

HWM: I know. I just thought it would be a good reminder.

NAMID looks temporarily defeated.

Now, ladies, I have prepared a feast and I have asked you to enjoy it with me.

MG2: Where exactly would it please you for us to sit, most benevolent saviour, most glorious specimen of masculinity, most well-endowed master of all things?

NAMID: *(under her breath)* Oh for fuck's sake.

HWM: In a chair, obviously. Khh, ghg, ha, pssh, women.

NAMID: You took all the chairs, ya goddamn trash can!

HWM: Ooh.

NARRATOR: He looks around the room, and, for the first time in his entire life, notices something.

A long pause.

HWM: It seems we're short on chairs.

MG2 applauds, then stops, embarrassed.

NAMID: No.

HWM: No? How do you know that word?

NAMID: I know many things. And I know that we are not short on chairs. You're just using three when you only need one.

HWM: I beg your pardon?

MG2: You're using three when you only need one.

HWM: Three what?

NAMID & MG2: Chairs!

HWM: I'm not sure I understand.

NAMID: There are three people in this room.

HWM: Okay . . .

MG2: And there are three chairs.

HWM: Okay . . .

NAMID: So there are exactly enough chairs—

MG2: —for each of us to sit in.

NARRATOR: The Man is more confused than he has ever been before.

HWM: That's too bad about the chair shortage. I don't see any possible solution to this problem! But please, join me. I have prepared a great feast.

> *NAMID and MG2 crouch at the table and sit on invisible chairs. They sip and slurp an invisible feast.*

8

JUDEO-CHRISTIAN OVERLORDS: Meanwhile, in that same old classroom in that same old residential school in the same old so-not-distant-enough past . . .

FATHER ALOYSIUS: Joan.

SISTER AGNES: Joan

FATHER ALOYSIUS: We have some news.

SISTER AGNES: Terrible news.

NAMID: What is it? Is my family okay?

SISTER AGNES: Yes, they are fine. Our news is much, much worse.

FATHER ALOYSIUS: The band is breaking up.

SISTER AGNES: *(with reluctance)* On behalf of the Church, we would like to issue a formal apology.

FATHER ALOYSIUS: Apparently, we were wrong about this whole genocide thing.

SISTER AGNES: But rest assured, assimilation will continue for generations. The special kind of trauma we inflict knows no bounds.

FATHER ALOYSIUS: We have failed you, Joan. The band just never achieved the kind of success it deserved. It is time for you to return home.

NAMID: But this is my home. Why must I leave?

FATHER ALOYSIUS: Ours is not to reason why, ours is but to do and die and turn and face the strange ch-ch-changes.

Thunder.

SISTER AGNES: Don't speak a word about this . . . if you do, the floodwater will come for you. Remember now, God is watching.

FATHER ALOYSIUS: It is time for you to return to your savage tribe and educate them as we have educated you in the civilized way of the Lord and in the ways of rock and roll.

NAMID: Yes, Father. I am a child of the Lord our God, who died for my sins, and socialized with prostitutes and lepers more frequently than may be advisable. You and Sister Agnes have raised me up and shown me the way to paradise by the dashboard light and I am no longer dancing in the dark as I climb the long and steep stairway to heaven. I'll be on my way . . . as soon as I hear your apology.

SISTER AGNES: We already apologized.

NAMID: No, you said you'd like to apologize.

SISTER AGNES: Potato, potahto.

FATHER ALOYSIUS: One fish, two fish, red fish, blue fish.

NAMID: I am certain the floodwaters would love to hear all about what you have done here. How you cut my hair, took me from my family—

(*to* SISTER AGNES) —beat me—

(*to* FATHER ALOYSIUS) —raped me—

(*to both*) —changed my name, punished me for speaking my own language, and destroyed my connection to the land.

SISTER AGNES: Don't you dare tell the water any of that.

NAMID: That's the thing your people don't seem to understand, Sister: the water already knows.

Thunder. The rain begins to fall.

SISTER AGNES: We're suh . . . so . . . sah . . . sorrrrrrrrreeeeeeaaaahyyyey. We're sorry. Aren't we, Father?

FATHER ALOYSIUS: Yes. Deeply. We didn't know what we were doing. I'm not even a real priest—I'm Jewish.

NAMID: Thank you.

Beat.

Apology not accepted. But keep trying! It will likely take generations.

SISTER AGNES: But the flood! The waters will drown us.

NAMID: Hmm. I guess it's time to turn and face the strange ch-ch-changes. Now, how do I find my way home?

SISTER AGNES & FATHER ALOYSIUS: Your true name will guide you home.

NAMID: You gotta be fucking kidding me.

Thunder.

9

NARRATOR: Later that same evening, only a mere sixty years in the future, in that extremely equal, legendary, democratic castle:

THE SPEAKER OF THE HOUSE OF THE PAGAN GODS: My Queen, the men are ready.

THE DUCHESS: Oh yes!

NAMID: Oh noooo.

THE QUEEN: Oh-kay. I hope this round is better than the last round. That last round there were only two worthwhile men to choose from and, out of those two, neither of them could cook. One did look wonderful in handcuffs, though.

NAMID: Barf.

(*to audience*) Every year on my birthday, a group of men are paraded past me. Every year my mother says:

THE QUEEN: It is time for you to find your own furniture!

NAMID: And every year I say—

(*to THE QUEEN*) I don't want my own furniture, ya stupid whore!

THE QUEEN: Well, you can't sit on mine and freeload for the rest of your life!

NAMID: And so on and so forth until all the men are paraded past and all the men are—usually—rejected.

ACCOUTREMENTS and FURNISHINGS walk down an imaginary runway, over and over, in assorted sexy vogue-y poses. NAMID shakes her head, every time.

THE QUEEN: Off with their heads! Off. With. Their. Heads.

NAMID: She says this every time.

THE DUCHESS: Must it ALLLLLLLuh-ways be beheading? Every time?

NAMID: She asks this every time.

THE QUEEN: Yes. It must always be beheading, every time.

NAMID: This happens every time. The beheading—usually—comes next.

FURNISHINGS and ACCOUTREMENTS are reluctantly prepared by THE DUCHESS and NAMID for a beheading while a distant hand drum begins to beat. THE SPEAKER OF THE HOUSE OF THE PAGAN GODS, GITCHE MANITOU'S RECORD PLAYER, JUDEO-CHRISTIAN OVERLORDS, and NARRATOR merge together to form one voice, a voice that whispers "Namid" in gentle rhythm with the drum.

But not this time.

As the drum sounds nearer and nearer, THE DUCHESS raises her axe high in the air. Just as she is about to swing it down on FURNISHINGS's head, the hand drum beat intensifies, and:

Gibichiwebinan!

Everyone stares at NAMID in shock.

Enough.

The drums and voices stop.

THE QUEEN: Hhhhwhhhat is the meaning of this? Speaking that disgusting language? In my castle?

NAMID: That "disgusting" language is the language of our ancestors.

THE QUEEN: It is a language of savages, of deadbeats, of alcoholics, of criminals—

NAMID: Of parents who don't know how to love because they never experienced love themselves. What did they do to you there, Mother?

THE QUEEN: I don't want to talk about it.

NAMID: But you must. If we don't learn from the past, the future will take its revenge.

THE QUEEN: Nonsense. Have you made your choice of furnishings or accoutrements?

NAMID: Yes.

NAMID selects both FURNISHINGS and ACCOUTREMENTS.

THE QUEEN: Two?

THE DUCHESS: But that one's mine!

She points at FURNISHINGS. FURNISHINGS waves.

THE QUEEN: *(impressed)* It seems I've underestimated you. I chose two men as well when I was your age.

NAMID: I have made my decision, Mother. I present to the kingdom my men: Furnishings and Accoutrements. And by the power vested in me, by the magic of my wand, I hereby free them, and all men in this kingdom.

NAMID hands FURNISHINGS to THE DUCHESS. They reunite in a warm embrace.

THE QUEEN: What the—

NAMID: And as for you, Mother.

THE DUCHESS, FURNISHINGS, and ACCOUTREMENTS grab THE QUEEN and hold her in place.

THE QUEEN: What are you doing? Off with her head!

NAMID: No, Mother. You have no power here anymore. I have chosen my furniture and I am Queen now.

Thunder.

I had hoped you would have a change of heart. I had hoped the waters would not come for you. But here they are . . . listen!

The sound of distant rain, drums, and voices.

THE DUCHESS: You should have been nicer, Sister dictator.

NAMID: You should have been kinder, Mother warlord.

THE DUCHESS: You took everything from me! You enslaved my husband and you embargoed all the cake while my nation starved. For many years I resented you for it. I probably always will.

NAMID: You gave me everything and nothing all at the same time, and for many years I resented you for it . . . but not anymore. You inherited desolation and made of it what you could, however corrupt it might have been. I am proud to be your daughter, and proud to be Queen. I forgive you, Mother. Miigwetch.

A downpour of water falls from the sky.

THE QUEEN: Well. Doesn't this make for great television?

And THE QUEEN drowns.

10

NARRATOR: Friday night. Date night. The Man and his women continue to feast in a terrible, ominous silence.

The sound of buffalo hooves beating across the land.

NAMID: A boy once told me to call them bison, not buffalo. He told me that the early settlers mistook them for the same species that reside in Asia and Africa, but that the settlers were wrong. I don't think about him very often anymore . . . but to this day I am careful to call them bison.

Drum beats. Whispered voices. When the drums reach their peak, the women look at one another and rise. The revolution begins.

What do we want?

MG2: Equal human rights!

NAMID: When do we want it?

MG2: As soon as it's convenient!

NAMID: No! Now! What do we want?

MG2: Chairs?

NAMID: And when do we want it?

MG2: Ideally, as soon as possible!

NAMID: No! Now!

NAMID & MG2: Chairs now! Equal rights now! Chairs now! Equal rights now! Now! Now! Now! Now! Now! Now! Now! Now!

Chairs soon! Equal rights when it's convenient! Chairs soon! Equal rights when it's convenient! Soon! When it's convenient! Now! Now! Now! Now! Now!

They chant their different chants simultaneously until their discord turns to harmony.

HWM: Is something the matter?

NAMID: Aye, it is you, sir, who are the matter.

MG2: Sir, you have burdened us with your shackles for too long.

NAMID: Our children cry and you do nothing.

MG2: Our children die and you do nothing.

NAMID: The flood is upon us and here you sit, useless, forgotten, and easily sunburnt.

HWM: Ah, uh-huh, mm-hmm, yes, oui, oui, oui, I see, I see. You see, it's, ah, the crying thing? I can explain, see, it's just science. It's like, see: I literally cannot hear our children cry. You gotta understand, when a woman gives birth, there's a chemical process that happens in their brains and they just, like, bond with the baby. A baby's cry is at a frequency that only women can hear. Even if I wanted to, I couldn't hear it.

MG2: I wanted no more children. You forced yourself upon me and gave me one anyway.

HWM: *Actually*, that's a funny story. Simple science again, nothing complicated, but still probably beyond your comprehension. Now, it's like this: when a woman is raped, and I mean really raped, "rape" I mean, not just "rape-rape," the body has special ways of shutting that whole thing down.

NAMID: We will no longer pick your cotton. We will no longer bear your children.

MG2: Nevermore shall we cook your feasts. Nevermore shall we rescue your teabags from the Assiniboine River after your imperialist temper tantrums.

NAMID: No more fur for your pasty feet. No more bannock for your bloated belly.

Thunder. Drums. Voices. Bison. Rain.

MG2: The flood is upon us!

HWM: Then we must move.

NAMID: We will move. You will stay behind.

HWM: But the floodwaters will drown me!

MG2: You will stay behind.

NAMID: You will stay behind and drown in the waters that have come to cleanse the land. You who have stolen so much. You who have taken more than your fair share.

MG2: You who breaks bones and breaks hearts and sits in too many chairs!

NAMID: This ahki is ours. This zahgidiwin is ours. Everything under the geesis and ahnung is ours, not yours!

MG2: But do not doubt I love you, my gentle, humble captor.

NAMID: Gi zah gin, my most cherished, most oblivious, most mansplaining serial killer.

MG2: But you understand, you must die.

NAMID: You understand. You must die. So that we can live.

MG2: We can speak now.

NAMID: You understand.

MG2: You must die. Thank you for everything.

NAMID: (*sarcastically*) Miigwetch! I will offer the elders tobacco and ask them to pray for you to Creator.

NAMID and MG2 clasp hands and summon the reckoning waters of the storm.

MG2: Our Father or Mother who art in heaven, hallowed be thy name.

NAMID: Yea, though I walk through the valley of the shadow of death, I shall fear no evil. For thou art with me. Thy suspiciously phallic rod and staff, they comfort me.

NAMID & MG2: Thou preparest a table before me in the presence of mine enemies.

Thunder. Lightning. Rain. Bison. Drums. The flood arrives and destroys the HWM. The water dissipates with the drums, the rain, the bison, the thunder, and the lightning, until there is nothing but the gentle sound of birds chirping.

NARRATOR: And the memory of the Heterosexual White Male is washed away like chalk on a sidewalk in the rain.

A long pause.

MG2: Now what?

NAMID: Now we are free.

MG2: Where do we go?

NAMID: Anywhere we want.

MG2: At home, they called me Agnes.

NAMID: At home, they called me . . .

A shooting star dances across the sky.

. . . Namid.

11

Darkness.

NARRATOR: Out of the darkness there is light.

Light.

Out of the light there is certainty.

Certainty.

Out of that certainty is a woman.

NAMID *enters.*

She stands centre stage, right where she belongs.

She waves.

Out of that woman's womb are people.

Enter HWM, MG2, FURNISHINGS, *and* ACCOUTREMENTS.

They are, as yet, uncertain.

*Lana Del Rey's cover of Leonard Cohen's "Chelsea Hotel #2"
begins to play on* GITCHE MANITOU'S RECORD PLAYER. NAMID
*sits and spreads her legs far apart across three chairs. The stage
directions that follow are interspersed between verses, with the
final line of the song playing immediately before the last stage
direction.*

*She makes herself as small as possible. The others watch her,
waiting.*

She takes up as much space as she needs

She stands. Together, they fix HWM's *hair and makeup.*

He becomes an object of great value.

Together, they smear at their own makeup.

Together, they undress.

Together, they hold their breath for as long as they can. One by one, they release it. When the last breath is exhaled, there is darkness, light, and certainty.

The end.

THE MILLENNIAL MALCONTENT

ERIN SHIELDS

ACKNOWLEDGEMENTS

In addition to those who participated in the original production, I would like to thank Richard Rose, Andrea Romaldi, David Jansen, Tamara Bernier Evans, and Peter Hinton for dramaturgical support throughout the process. Also, a huge thank you to Sir John Vanbrugh, who's play *The Provok'd Wife* inspired this piece.

PLAYWRIGHT'S NOTE

I fell in love with *The Provoked Wife* by Sir John Vanbrugh when I played the role of Lady Fanciful at Rose Bruford College in London, England. On the surface, there is a lightness to the text—a playful banter concerning marriage, the morality of the sexes, romantic pursuits, disguises, mistaken identities, and drunken drag. In short, all the ingredients of a solid Restoration Comedy. At the same time, however, there is a darker comedy at play: a vain, self-deluded woman is shamelessly ridiculed; a virtuous wife is trapped in an abusive marriage; a reckless bawd is cuckolded and spirals into self-loathing. The tension between these two modes of comedy provides space for satire and critique of the social dynamics at play. Vanbrugh does not pass moral judgment on the actions of his characters, but rather invites us to laugh at both the light and the dark, to find pleasure in the pain of the characters and, I believe, in ourselves.

Youth culture today is still a world of two very different narratives. There is the light, crafted, online, public persona in which people celebrate their victories, proclaim their social and political alliances, and ridicule mainstream "bad guys." Occasionally there is a pronouncement of loss: a break up, a death, a cry for help. But even those cries seem somehow superficial, a scratching at the surface of the terrifying complexity of what it is to be human. This curated participation in online forums fosters an isolation which can give way to desperate longing—a longing for honest connection, a longing for self-fulfilling work with substantial remuneration, a longing for alcoholic obliteration, a longing for individualism and love. My goal with *The Millennial Malcontent* was to craft a contemporary Restoration Comedy that would speak directly to the social dynamics of our time in order to both reflect and critique the world we live in today.

As I wrote and rewrote and rewrote *The Millennial Malcontent*, I got further and further from the original play. I changed the genders of most of the characters, chose a different protagonist, put the characters in situations that would be immediately recognizable to today's millennials. What remains of the source material are those two layers of comedy. On the surface, there is a light, playful banter of romantic intrigues, entrepreneurial exploits, and over the top fashion choices that poke fun at the social mores of contemporary hipster culture. But there is also a painful longing at the core of all of these characters; an exposed loneliness as each one strives for something that is unattainable in their world.

I would like to thank Tarragon Theatre for its support throughout the writing process. Specifically, Richard Rose, Peter Hinton, Andrea Romaldi, David Jansen, and Tamara Bernier Evans for their dramaturgical input. Thanks also to the Canada Council for supporting the writing process with a playwright-in-residence grant. And finally, a personal thank you to my family—Gideon, Olive, and Tallulah—for putting up with my numerous trips from Montreal to work on the play.

"EVERYONE IS HAPPY": PERFORMING ADAPTATION, IRONY, AND GENDER IN *THE MILLENNIAL MALCONTENT*

KAILIN WRIGHT

> "Everyone is happy.
> Everyone is fine.
> Everyone is posting things on each other's things all the time.
> EVERYONE IS HAPPY!"
> —Erin Shields, *The Millennial Malcontent*

The refrain "everyone is happy" rings out through the theatre at the end of Erin Shields's *The Millennial Malcontent* (2017), which adapts a Restoration Comedy to contemporary millennial culture. As the closing line suggests, through its over-assertion of contentedness, Shields's play examines what makes its millennial characters so unhappy with marriage, work, social media, and themselves. According to Rosebud1776 on *Urban Dictionary*, an online reference source popular with millennials, the millennial generation was born between 1981 and 2001; despite this twenty-year birth range, millennials are defined and united by their transformation of digital communication and identity. Shields's play suggests that millennials also value gender fluidity, organic food, drugs, social media, and ironic clothing. In adapting John Vanbrugh's *The Provoked Wife* (1697), Shields's *The Millennial Malcontent* layers performances of millennial culture with a seventeenth-century comedy about marriage and gender. "My goal," Shields explains in her playwright's note, "was to craft a contemporary Restoration Comedy that would speak directly to the social dynamics of our time in order to both reflect and critique the world we live in today."

Shields's plays often adapt past works from a feminist or gender perspective and *The Millennial Malcontent* is no different. In *The Provoked Wife*, Sir John Brute is, as his name suggests, a miserable, abusive, and unloving man who drives his wife Lady Brute to infidelity. Although Vanbrugh's play is first and foremost a comedy, it also depicts an unhappy wife's pain and limited options to escape her marriage. In fact, because the play can be seen to condone women's rights and adultery, *The Provoked Wife* was controversial at the time.[1] It remains so today, but for different reasons. According to *Globe and Mail* reviewer J. Kelly Nestruck, "you've probably never seen" *The Provoked Wife* because it has likely not "ever had a staging in Canada outside of theatre schools." While Nestruck does not hypothesize why, other critics have pointed out that the play's appeal may be limited because contemporary audiences find it hard to laugh at the violence of its male protagonist (Billington). *The Millennial Malcontent* reverses the primary gender roles in *The Provoked Wife* in order to question how the gendered stereotypes of female chastity or vanity and male bravery or lewdness are performed today. In Shields's adaptation, Moxy is a brutish wife who drives her adoring husband Johnny into the arms of Faith.

In *A Theory of Adaptation*, Linda Hutcheon explains that adaptations provide the pleasure of a palimpsest because audiences' experience of an adaptation is layered with their previous experience with the source material. Hutcheon adds, however, that an adaptation can be viewed separately from and without any prior knowledge of the source. In keeping with Hutcheon's theory of adaptation, audiences need not be familiar with the source material to understand Shields's adaptation, but knowledge of *The Provoked Wife* does offer more moments of comedy. Nestruck goes so far as to suggest that *The Millennial Malcontent* requires a prior knowledge of *The Provoked Wife* to understand the comedy and social critique. The opening line

---

1   For more on *The Provoked Wife*'s stage history and critical reception, see Antony Coleman's edition of the play.

of *The Millennial Malcontent*, for instance, is a humorous update to Vanbrugh's play, which begins with Sir John Brute declaring, "What cloying meat is love, when matrimony's the sauce to it." In keeping with the exaggerated feelings of a Restoration Comedy, Moxy's blunt statement "Marriage sucks!" sets the tone of Shields's play. Moxy finds herself stuck in a marriage that she finds boring, which is perhaps the worst feeling that she can imagine.

The play presents gender, like marriage, as another superficial performance to be donned or cast off as easily as a pair of skinny jeans. In fact, the play's central fool character, named Charm (a gender-swapped take on Vanbrugh's meddling Lady Fancyful), is the personification of curated masculinity. Johnny and his best "bro" Heartfree immediately poke fun at Charm—a narcissistic "bro" who assumes that "every woman is lining up to get with him"—because of his heavy-handed self-identification as the male heartthrob. Later in the play, Moxy dresses up in Charm's clothes and acts like an oversexed "brooooo!!!" In a more physical assault on performances of toxic, hypersexual masculinity, Moxy and Raz chase a man in a penis costume off the stage at the end of the third act, taking their critique of gender norms and patriarchy to the extreme as they threaten to "punch him in the face and push him off a bridge."

Moxy's brutishness (to use the language from the source material) is an extension of the gender critique because she rejects the stereotype of the faithful, timid, and agreeable wife. She literally attacks a phallus and challenges the notion of marriage as a life goal. The character list describes her as "an irritable provocateur" who is "independently wealthy": she does not need her husband's emotional, financial, or sexual support. Her moxie, however, reveals itself to be, at least in part, a veil by the play's end when Moxy is surprised that her devoted husband was tempted to cheat on her with their friend Faith. By presenting gender, radical bitchiness, and even faithfulness as flimsy performances, the play asks, what is authentic?

Restoration Comedy's interplay of light and dark comedy is a fitting form for Shields's social critique because it enhances the discord between surface and depth in millennial culture. While at first glance, Shields's characters seem like Restoration stock characters-turned-superficial millennials, with aptronyms like Moxy, Faith, Charm, and Heartfree, the play reveals them to be more than their social media profiles. As the play develops, these characters share their own experiences with the deep loneliness of always being connected online. In the Playwright's Note, Shields explains how millennial culture participates in two foil narratives: the happy, successful, online public performance of one's life as well as the darker, lonely experience that comes from a world where we communicate "virtually." Shields explores how these two lived narratives are interrelated because "curated participation in online forums fosters an isolation" and "a longing for honest connection." In *The Millennial Malcontent*, the constant demands to perform happiness and hipness make the characters unhappy and even (in Charm's case) uncool.

Equipped with a deepened understanding of the stock characters' interiority, the audience experiences the play's final lines as layered: we can read the deeper pain underneath the protestations that "everyone is happy." Charm, the social-media guru with his own YouTube channel and mass of followers, sits at a synthesizer and sings: "Everyone is happy. Everyone is fine. Everyone is posting things about having a fabulous time. Nobody's lonely. No one's upset. No one's expecting things to be constantly laced with regret." These lyrics, however, are ironic and the second verse explains:

Sometimes I'm tempted
to think the world is just unfair,
to leave me stranded with my dreams
and feeling unaware.
I stare into the mirror
and feel like a disgrace.
It's then that I remember
to take a photo of my face.

The act of taking "a photo of my face"—a selfie—brings the singer Charm out of a more honest confession of his feelings and back to the false performance that,

Everything is awesome.
Everything is cool.
Everything is happening
And nobody looks like a fool.

Charm may say that "nobody looks like a fool," but he acts as the play's archetypal wise fool that delivers the play's final message.

Each character listens to Charm's song "in his/her own space" as they are joined together in their individual isolation, listening "without irony" and "even encourag[ing] the audience to join in or clap." It is a climactic performance of irony because the seemingly light vehicles—the speaker (a ridiculed fool character), form (a novice song with a synthesizer), and medium (a streamed video)—express a dark tenor. In this final moment where each character listens alone, they are finally joined by their shared experience of a darker loneliness that lurks beneath millennials' social media posts, selfies, and followers. Charm's song invites empathy for the characters' malcontent and the dark comedy gives weight to the insistence that "EVERYONE IS HAPPY." In *The Millennial Malcontent*, Shields exposes a paradox of the millennial generation where everyone looks, but no one is, happy.

WORKS CITED

Billington, Michael. "*The Provoked Wife* Review—When Wedlock Turns to Deadlock." Review of *The Provoked Wife*, by Sir John Vanbrugh, directed by Phillip Breen, the Swan, Stratford-upon-Avon. *The Guardian*, 13 May 2019, https://www.theguardian.com/stage/2019/may/13/the-provoked-wife-review-the-swan-stratford-upon-avon. Accessed 2 Dec. 2021.

Hutcheon, Linda. *A Theory of Adaptation*. Routledge, 2006.

Nestruck, J. Kelly. "*Millennial Malcontent*: Updated Play Makes Little Sense on Its Own." Review of *The Millennial Malcontent*, by Erin Shields, directed by Peter Hinton, Tarragon Theatre, Toronto. *The Globe and Mail*, 10 Mar. 2017, https://www.theglobeandmail.com

/arts/theatre-and-performance/theatre-reviews/millennial-malcontent-updated-play-makes-little-sense-on-its-own/article34265367/. Accessed 2 Dec. 2021.

Rosebud1776. "Millennial." *Urban Dictionary*, 8 Jan. 2017, https://www.urbandictionary.com/define.php?term=Millennial. Accessed 2 Dec. 2021.

Vanbrugh, Sir John. *The Provoked Wife*. Edited by Antony Coleman, Manchester UP, 1982.

The Millennial Malcontent received its English-language premiere at Tarragon Theatre in the Mainspace from February 28 to April 9, 2017 with the following cast:

Moxy: Liz Peterson
Johnny: Reza Sholeh
Heartfree: James Daly
Mimi: Amelia Sargisson
Charm: Frank Cox-O'Connell
Raz: Alicia Richardson
Faith: Rong Fu
Teasel: Natasha Mumba

Directed by: Peter Hinton
Projection designer: Howard Davis
Lighting designer: Jennifer Lennon
Sound designer: Lyon Smith
Set and costume designer: Joanna Yu
Stage manager: Marinda de Beer
Projection coordinator: David Costello
Apprentice stage manager: Troy Taylor
Directing apprentice: Robynne Harder
Script coordinator: Haritha Popuri
Cutter: Laura Delchiaro

CHARACTERS

Moxy: (f) An irritable provocateur. Independently wealthy.
Johnny: (m) Her husband. A nice guy. NGO intern.
Heartfree: (m) Johnny's best friend. Also a nice guy. Music reviewer.
Mimi: (f) Visiting Québécoise student. Cousin to Charm. Filmmaker.
Charm: (m) Vain YouTube star.
Raz: (f) Computer programmer. Lesbian hip hop artist.
Faith: (f) In love with Johnny. Entrepreneur.
Teasel: (f) Friend of Faith. Master's student.

SETTING

An augmented present. Shades of Restoration Comedy should be visible through a thick veneer of contemporary hipster culture.

DESIGN

Design should be consciously self-referential and buzzing with current technology. Selfies and the idea of selfies should be present throughout. Music and art should be cool and subversive. Not pop culture. Millennial, hipster culture.

CASTING

Beautiful. Young. Culturally diverse.

ACT 1

SCENE 1—MARRIAGE SUCKS

MOXY: Marriage sucks.

The only thing worse than marriage
is talking about marriage,
and talking about marriage
is all he wants to do.

"Isn't it nice," he says,
"isn't it cozy and calm and reassuring to know
we're in it for life."

Snore.

So why did I get married?
I thought a wedding would feel like something;
that I would vibrate with life and beauty
and people would say:
"Look at her vibrate with life and beauty."
I thought the joy of that feeling
and the reflection of the joy of that feeling
would pierce the deadening buzz
of traffic and air conditioning
and getting whatever I want.

Why did I get married so young?
In part, to piss off my parents,
but mostly for the photographs.

If you wait to get married, you have to manufacture youth
so you can tell your future self
that you were in your prime.
The effort of disguising age is so revoltingly transparent—
the diets, the hair colour, the skin creams.
Better to be young for posterity;
it takes so much less effort.

And the sperm, of course, there's the sperm.
Gotta book your sperm in advance
because good genes marry quickly
and who wants to take a chance on big ears
or a low IQ or a penchant for gambling or whiskey,
not that I want a kid right now,
but someday,
well,
you know.

My husband is attractive.
Most agree he's hot.
His parents are attractive too
and there's no sign of mental health issues,
early onset Alzheimer's, or cancers of any kind.
And he's clever enough.
Occasionally funny, even.
But marriage has made him so boring.

There's nothing he'd like more
than to order in and binge-watch a Netflix Original Series
curled up on the couch like a couple of cats,
licking each other's soft spots
and burrowing into a half-slumber
before dragging ourselves to the bathroom
to brush our teeth and tuck in till dawn
when he wakes with the sun to go for his run,
shower, and skip off to his unpaid internship.

And if he whiffs the scent of discontent,
he channels his nice-guy voice and says,
"We should talk about this."

I'd get rid of him altogether if I could bear
the inevitable conversations that would ensue.

Besides, it's much more fun this way.

> JOHNNY *enters with a cup of coffee and a flower in a vintage,*
> *handmade vase.*

JOHNNY: Happy anniversary!

MOXY: Has it been a year already?

JOHNNY: I made breakfast-in-bed.

MOXY: I thought I smelled something unique.

JOHNNY: I'm experimenting with shakshuka.

MOXY: Hope you added lots of hot sauce.

JOHNNY: The recipe didn't call for—

MOXY: Shakshuka's bland unless you lay on the heat.

JOHNNY: Get back to bed and I'll bring it in.

> JOHNNY *exits.*

> MOXY *gets dressed.*

MOXY: (*to audience*) He's excited now.
Thinks we'll slurp tomatoey eggs under the blankets

and have a considered conversation
about our marriage.
Where we've been and where we're going.
Maybe vision-board our hopes for the future.

JOHNNY enters with the plates.

JOHNNY: I hope I didn't go overboard.
But you ask for heat, you get heat!

MOXY: Well, let me know how that goes.

JOHNNY: But I thought—

MOXY: I've got brunch plans already.

JOHNNY: Moxy—

MOXY: Later, sweet cheeks.

JOHNNY: I was just trying to make something you like.

MOXY: You have no idea what I like.

JOHNNY: You liked the Indian I made yesterday.

MOXY: What I liked yesterday, I don't like today.
And what I like today,
I can't be bothered to like tomorrow.

JOHNNY: I could cut up some fruit.

MOXY: You're so accommodating.

JOHNNY: Have I done something wrong?

MOXY: You tell me.

JOHNNY: What's the matter? We should talk.

MOXY: Anything but that.

JOHNNY: You married me for love.

MOXY: You married me for money.

JOHNNY: Hey!

MOXY: We both got what we bargained for,
so let's just leave it at that.

JOHNNY: I think we should talk about this.

    MOXY exits.

We should talk about this!

(to audience) I didn't marry for money.
I'm not the type of guy
who would marry someone for money.
Although she does have money
and that hasn't been a bad thing
for my student loans.

We met in Ghana on a volunteer mission
coaching teenagers from Winnipeg through their
traumatic awakenings to the ugliness of poverty.
We'd stay out all night in the expat bar
and lose ourselves in the ocean,
swimming under the stars.
It was beautiful.

I was attracted to her spunk.
To her instinct for subversion.
She dared two guys who grabbed her ass
to make out with one another.
She wore a headscarf to the airport
and didn't remove her pocket change.
She talked her way out of a women's studies exam
by feigning an abortion.
There's nothing more attractive
than an aggressive sense of irony,
but day in and day out . . .

To be perfectly honest, I thought my charm would round her edge.
I'm a really nice guy.
I'm a good-looking guy.
I'm a gentle guy.
I'm an honest guy with an impressive record collection
who knows how to cook and play the euphonium
and analyze his feelings and share his feelings
and listen to other people share their feelings.
What woman isn't interested in building a life with a guy like that?
But everything I do,
everything I say,
seems to drive her crazy.
Even looking at me starts to irritate her,
so rather than critique the social hypocrisies of our time,
she has, instead, turned her attention to critiquing me.

I'm using every bit of intellectual, emotional,
and spiritual focus I have to stay honest.
But who knows how long this good guy will last
when I'm constantly pushed to the edge of
what any reasonable man can reasonably tolerate.

Enter HEARTFREE.

HEARTFREE: Hey, bro.

JOHNNY: Hey, bro.

HEARTFREE: You look pissed.

JOHNNY: I am.

HEARTFREE: With me?

JOHNNY: My wife.

HEARTFREE: Screw wives.
Especially yours.

JOHNNY: Yo, bro, I can't handle ironic misogyny today.

HEARTFREE: Sorry, man, it just really winds me up
to see how she spins you around.
Doesn't she know how lucky she is?
I mean, you're a nice guy.

JOHNNY: I know.

HEARTFREE: Like, a really nice guy
with a prestigious unpaid internship
at an impressive NGO.

JOHNNY: I know.

HEARTFREE: I mean, you're trying to start your own charity
to rescue toddlers from toothpicks,
what more does she want?!

JOHNNY: Yeah, well, it's actually Toothpicks for Toddlers.

HEARTFREE: Right, yeah, to help with oral hygiene in developing—

JOHNNY: Actually, the idea is to set up a toothpick factory in a developing country, export the toothpicks to a developed country, and invest the profit back into the original developing country to care for toddlers.

HEARTFREE: You're the best.

JOHNNY: Thanks.

HEARTFREE: You need to cheat on your wife.

JOHNNY: Don't say that.

HEARTFREE: I miss my buddy, bro.

JOHNNY: I'm still here.

HEARTFREE: Yeah, but you're all frowns and rainclouds.

JOHNNY: And sacrificing my integrity
would only make it worse.

HEARTFREE: But it's like she wants you to.

JOHNNY: I know.

HEARTFREE: It's like she's prodding you.

JOHNNY: I know.

HEARTFREE: It's like she's daring you to sleep with someone else.

JOHNNY: I've been thinking she might have abandonment issues or some sort of childhood trauma.

HEARTFREE: The only trauma I see,
is the trauma she's inflicting on you.
There is divorce.

JOHNNY: I don't have the stomach for a word like that.

HEARTFREE: Or the money.

JOHNNY: Money means nothing to me.

HEARTFREE: You were up to your eyeballs in debt.

JOHNNY: Like, I never think about money.

HEARTFREE: And now that you're back to zero,
those eyeballs are free to wander.

JOHNNY: What are you talking about?

HEARTFREE: And those eyeballs have set their sights
on something sweet.

JOHNNY: I have no idea—

HEARTFREE: On one who thinks you hate her
even though I know you don't.

JOHNNY: You mean . . . Faith.

HEARTFREE: Funny how you guessed it.

JOHNNY: Oh, I . . .

HEARTFREE: You blush when you see her,
then you pry yourself away,
then you turn back to tell a joke

while she's cleaning off your table
and you're sitting with your MacBook
and you stew yourself in trying
not to let her know you're looking.

JOHNNY: I never thought I'd be the type of guy
who'd consider cheating on his wife.

HEARTFREE: You never thought you'd have a wife
who'd push you straight toward it.

JOHNNY: That's what I'm scared of.

HEARTFREE: Faith is into you, bro.

JOHNNY: But I'm no flirt.
Especially when I don't intend
to please her with resolve.

HEARTFREE: You're the best.

JOHNNY: I just can't bear to watch women suffer.

HEARTFREE: Careful or you'll start to sound like Charm.

JOHNNY: That bad?

HEARTFREE: Have you seen what he's done to his hair?
Shaved flowers into the sides
and poofed it up on top.

JOHNNY: He's decided every woman is lining up to get with him.

HEARTFREE: And whatever they post confirms it.

JOHNNY: If they make fun of how ridiculous he is,
he thinks they're laughing at his jokes.

HEARTFREE: If they're rude,
he says they're trying to cover up their passion.

JOHNNY: Even if they unfriend him,
he says they're playing hard to get.

HEARTFREE: He's decided everything all women do online
has everything to do with him.

JOHNNY: And he pities all men
because he thinks we're jealous.

They laugh.

HEARTFREE: Hey, is that shakshuka.

JOHNNY: Go for it.

HEARTFREE: You're the best.

He shovels in a mouthful.

The hot sauce hits.

Music.

SCENE 2—HOW DO I LOOK THIS MORNING?

Lights up on CHARM admiring himself in the mirror.

RAZ is fixing CHARM's computer.

MIMI watches them both.

CHARM: How do I look this morning?

RAZ: Like shit.

CHARM: Excuse me?

RAZ: I mean, like a really good shit.

CHARM: Thank you, Raz!

RAZ: Hey, you asked.

CHARM: And I didn't anticipate such an insulting response
from my technical support service technician.

RAZ: Jokes, baby, jokes.

CHARM: Ha ha ha.

RAZ: Look, I could go if you find my presence to be too insulting.

CHARM: No. No no no.
Fix my computer.

In the future, I'd just invite you to think
about the object of your vicious sense of humour.
You know how sensitive I am.
That I take everything to heart.
Even things that I know are impossible,
so think, next time, please think
before abusing me with your irony.

RAZ: Sure thing.

She winks at MIMI.

CHARM: Where's my other mirror?
I need a francophone opinion.

MIMI: What do I know about beauty?
Nothing, perhaps.
But in my opinion,
I think you look better than ever before in your life.

CHARM: You see?
Raz?
Direct.
Honest.
And we all know the Québécoise are too rude to flatter.

MIMI: Flatter?
What is this word?

CHARM: You see, Raz?

RAZ: Oh, I see plenty from where I'm sitting.

She winks at MIMI.

CHARM: Aren't you done yet?

RAZ: Just clearing out the porn.

CHARM: What? I—what?

RAZ: Your porn's slowing down your os.

CHARM: Is there any purity left in a world
where smut can download itself!

MIMI: You, cousin, are the purity.

CHARM: Thank you, Mimi.

MIMI: You fill the world with the handsome beauty.

CHARM: Biscotti?

MIMI: Merci.

CHARM: I'm so glad you've finally come for a visit.

MIMI: My mother thought I should practise the language of the overbearing culture.

CHARM: Cousine.

MIMI: Cousin.

Bisous.

RAZ: Gimme your phone.

CHARM: Sigh.

RAZ: You want it to synch or what?

CHARM hands over his phone.

Passcode.

CHARM: Sigh.

CHARM holds up his thumb.

RAZ touches CHARM's thumb to the phone to open it.

CHARM rolls his eyes at RAZ for MIMI's benefit.

RAZ winks at MIMI again.

MIMI giggles.

Have you ever been in love, Mimi?

MIMI: Oui.

CHARM: But it ended?

MIMI: Oui.

CHARM: And you suffered?

MIMI: Oui oui oui.

CHARM: I'm glad I've avoided it so far.
I mean there are women out there.
Women in the world at large.
Women with charm.
Women with beauty.
Women with intelligence, humour and creativity,
but I've never come across a woman
I could call the "full package."
If I did, I think there'd still be something missing.
That's just the way I am.
I demand a lot for myself.
Some might say too much.
In fact, high standards are one of the many crosses
I struggle to bear on a daily basis.
But could I love?
Yes.
I could love deeply.
Extraordinarily deeply.
Especially if it were possible to create that woman myself.

MIMI: Oui.

CHARM: You know in some ways, that's what I'm doing with my videos.
I'm attempting to create what doesn't exist;
a perfection only art can achieve.

MIMI: If I were not related to you by the blood,
I would gladly be that woman.
And I would give you all the thing in the world
like spontaneous present,
and spontaneous love song,
and spontaneous sexual favour.
I would not eat, not sleep, not live for thinking only of you.
I would hang myself, drown myself,
cut my heart from my very chest
and chew it slowly with my very mouth
while playing a lonely fugue on the violin
to prove my love to you.

CHARM: You are so . . . expressive, Mimi.

MIMI: Thank you.

CHARM: Cupcake?

MIMI: Merci.

RAZ: You're good to go.

CHARM: How much do I—

RAZ: Taken care of, babe.
You just sent me an e-transfer.

CHARM: You went into my—

RAZ: Thanks for the tip, by the way.

CHARM: Get out of here.

RAZ: (*to* MIMI) Isn't he generous.

MIMI: Ben oui.

RAZ: (*passing* MIMI *her number*) Let me know if you need anyone to show you around while you're here.

CHARM: Get out!

> *RAZ exits winking one more time at* MIMI.

MIMI: She is very nice.

CHARM: As nice as a festering wound,
but she's the only one who can ensure
all my platforms are running smoothly.

MIMI: You must get the fan message all the time.

CHARM: Especially after that last video.
I took my followers to a whole new level:

> *Channelling his video persona:*

"You ever, like, feel kinda, like, you know, like . . . down?
Well . . . don't:"

MIMI: Inspiré!

CHARM: That's what it's all about.
Inspiring real people to be themselves and—

MIMI: What is it?

CHARM: I've just had an idea.
For my next video.
Remember how you were suggesting
that I need to do something different,
something unexpected,
something no one would ever associate with me?

MIMI: You want to use the tiger!

CHARM: No. I want to use Real People.

MIMI: Pardon?

CHARM: We will gather a group of them,
a whole chorus of Real People
and at the end of my song,
the Real People will be dancing behind me
like Real People.

MIMI: How do Real People dance?

CHARM: Not very well,
which will not only highlight my message
of inclusivity and internal beauty,
but it will also make me look good.

MIMI: Incroyable!

CHARM: Now, the Real People will need to be Culturally Diverse.

MIMI: Why?

CHARM: To show my dedication to intersectionality.
And we'll need a Real Fat Person.

And a Real Disabled Individual in a Real Wheelchair.
And a Real Muslim Woman in a Real Niqab.

MIMI: But how will we verify her identity?

CHARM: And as the camera pans out,
we see there are more and more and more Real People
and all of those Real People are dancing to my song.
And an aerial view reveals that the Real People are dancing
in the shape of my face.
And when the Real People who make the shape of my mouth
bend at the hip, it looks like my big mouth in my big head
is singing my song.

A ding from his cellphone.

Here we go again.

(reading) "As a friend of a friend who friended you once,
my feed is constantly overflowing with your "content."
I am a Master's student studying self-performance
and would welcome the opportunity to conduct
a deeper investigation of . . . you.
I am experimenting with a radical new form of discourse I call:
Talking Face-to-Face.
If you'd like to engage with me in this practice,
meet me at the Farmer's Market in an hour."

MIMI: Incroyable!
Let's go.

CHARM: Mimi, Mimi, Mimi.
I realize you are new to the world of fans and super fans and the like,
but doesn't anything in this message sound suspicious to you?

MIMI: Suspicious?

CHARM: Give you pause?

MIMI: Paws?

CHARM: This talking Face-to-Face.

MIMI: Ah oui!
Pardon?

CHARM: To me, this smacks of a fan who cannot contain her passion.

MIMI: Ben oui!

CHARM: A fan with a desperate yearning for physical proximity to her idol.

MIMI: Ben oui!

CHARM: She may even have designs to ravish me.

MIMI: Ben oui oui oui!

CHARM: There is no satisfaction in taking advantage of vulnerable women.

MIMI: I would argue, there is some satisfaction.

CHARM: Sigh.
Well, I suppose I have a craving for crepes anyway.

MIMI: Moi aussi!

CHARM: Cousine.

MIMI: Cousin!

Bisous.

CHARM: Let's go.

A blast of music.

ACT 2

SCENE 1—YOU CAME

Dance piece: I Love the Market.

- *buying organic meals*
- *smelling organic fruit*
- *sipping organic coffee*
- *filling baskets with local vegetables*

CHARM and MIMI arrive on the scooter.

TEASEL watches them.

TEASEL: You came.

CHARM: Let's just say you managed to pique my interest.

TEASEL: Good.

CHARM: No . . . good for you.
Not many fans manage to distinguish themselves from the crowd.

TEASEL: You're far more humble than I thought you were.

CHARM: I think you'll find I'm an extremely humble person.

TEASEL: Evidently.

CHARM: In fact, I'm probably the most humble person I know.

But I'm also extremely busy.

TEASEL: Well, thank you for sparing the time.

Beat.

CHARM: So, I assume you want to know about my artistic process?

TEASEL: Not particularly.

CHARM: Then I assume you want to know about my sources of inspiration?

TEASEL: Not really.

CHARM: Perhaps my formative years as an artist?

TEASEL: Nah.

CHARM: My sleeping habits?

TEASEL: Nope.

CHARM: Bathing rituals?

TEASEL: Nope.

CHARM: My skin cream regimen?

TEASEL: Amazing!

CHARM: What?

TEASEL: You truly fascinate me.

CHARM: I do?

TEASEL: Yes. You have me dying to know how you approach the performance of your identity.

CHARM: What are you talking about?

TEASEL: Are you trying to be ironic or sincere?

CHARM: Pardon me?

TEASEL: Because when I look at your posts and your videos
I can't help but think you're sending up
the tropes and corporate trappings of popular culture
by embodying its most grotesque elements.
And yet, there's not a trace of irony,
no crack in the mask to let us know you're joking
so I wonder if you really,
truly expect people to take you seriously.

CHARM: I assure you, I am always serious.

TEASEL: Fascinating.

CHARM: Most people think so.

TEASEL: It must take so much time.

CHARM: What?

TEASEL: Plucking and gelling and dying your hair,
stretching, creaming, injecting your skin,
choosing clothes that are such an outrageous mimicry
of anything actually fashionable or cool.
You've even managed to contort the way you walk,
the way you talk,
the way you sing your ridiculous songs

into some sort of affected convulsion.

CHARM: My followers—both male and female, I'll have you know—
deeply admire my artistry.

TEASEL: The women pity you.
The men are just taking the piss.

MIMI: *(aside)* Is this how they make love in this province?

TEASEL: What if I told you that all of your "fans,"
every single one of those "followers"
is only egging you on to see how far they can push you
down the road of self-humiliation.

CHARM: Why would anyone, other than you,
act in such a hateful way?

TEASEL: For a laugh.

CHARM: A laugh?!

TEASEL: It's hilarious to watch you fan your feathers
and strut yourself left, right, and centre.

CHARM: I'm on to you.

TEASEL: I'm just trying to help.

CHARM: Right.
You think you can humiliate me by saying
I don't know the difference between cool and uncool,
appropriate and inappropriate,
honest and dishonest,
but I am grounded enough in my own sense of self

to be able to respond to you with both clarity and compassion
to let you know that I know that you know
that you are simply
talking
BULLSHIT!

    CHARM storms off.

MIMI: You hear him?
Bullshit.

CHARM: Viens, Mimi!

    MIMI follows.

TEASEL: *(to audience)* I tried.
You saw me.
I tried.
But once a man's puffed up on thinking
he's something to think about,
that's it.
He's greasing his hair, trimming his beard,
sniffing his pits, and squeezing himself into skinny jeans.

The days of cave men are gone.
No more thumping chests,
fixing cars,
kicking balls at one another.
No more grunting salutations,
no more wrestling in the halls,
no more sweat-stained T-shirts
or eating competitions.

It's all been downhill since men started to articulate their feelings.
They're still not very good at it

but want to be congratulated for the effort
and there's no privacy any more.

The intuitive skill that made women the superior species
is gradually being diluted.
Men have begun to navigate the realm of emotional metaphor
and, like children learning to read,
their ears perk up when we start to spell out feelings
we didn't want them to hear.
They've started crying in elevators
and gossiping in bathrooms
and pinching their bodies into clothes
they tell one another look good.

    FAITH enters with a box of pastries.

FAITH: *(holding out a piece of Zwetschgendatschi)* Taste this.

TEASEL: Oh. Wow!

FAITH: Gluten-free, vegan Zwetschgendatschi.

TEASEL: What?

FAITH: Zwetschgendatschi.
Bavarian plum cake.

TEASEL: Tasty.

FAITH: Rosie's going to let me sell them at her stall next week.

TEASEL: Amazing.

FAITH: And I found a place in Costa Rica that's already set up for yoga retreats.

TEASEL: Now you just need to convince the housewives to book their flights.

FAITH: Kneed, Knit, Kneel.

TEASEL: What?

FAITH: The name of my company.

TEASEL: Say it again?

FAITH: Kneed, Knit, Kneel.
The "Kneed" is for my vegan baked goods,
the "Knit" is for my infinity scarves,
and the "Kneel" is for my—

TEASEL: Blow job delivery service?

FAITH: You're a jerk.

TEASEL: Come on, Faith. Kneel?!

FAITH: I needed another silent "K" N-word.
"K-need," "K-nit," "K-neel."

TEASEL: So you can snag the acronym KKK.

FAITH: Hey.

TEASEL: You should get on that domain name.

FAITH: All right, I—

TEASEL: I've got your byline:
"Not the KKK you're thinking of."

FAITH: Then help me think of a better one.

TEASEL: Or, "Kneed, Knit, Kneel: the *other* KKK."

FAITH: I helped you think of a thesis for your first master's degree.

TEASEL: Yes, but—

FAITH: And your second.

TEASEL: Fair play.

FAITH: How many masters' do you have now, Teasel?
Are we up to four or five?

TEASEL: The pursuit of knowledge is never a waste of time.

FAITH: Especially when it keeps you from dealing with the Real World.

TEASEL: I can deal with the Real World.

FAITH: And there's lots of jobs in the Real World for an expert in the performance of self-consciously constructed personal identity.

TEASEL: Hey.

FAITH: What are you doing here anyway?
I thought you said the market smelled
like dreadlocks and pubic hair.

TEASEL: I found another subject for my research.

FAITH: Poor guy.

TEASEL: You really won't pity this one.

FAITH: I pity them all.

TEASEL: You might know him actually.
I think he's a friend of Johnny's.

FAITH: . . . Johnny . . .

TEASEL: Oh, Faith, you gotta stop.

FAITH: What?

TEASEL: He's married.

FAITH: I know, but I can't help it.
It's physical.
And spiritual, in some way.
I just feel like we're, you know, like, connected.

TEASEL: He still won't cheat on her, will he?

FAITH: It's been a year since Moxy invited me to their wedding
and I saw Johnny for the first time.
I remember a feeling of true enlightenment,
like I was somehow connected to the Universe
and all the creatures in it.
Since that day, I've loved him more
than a vegan loves Tofurky.

TEASEL: I know.

FAITH: But he's cold to me, so cold.

TEASEL: All men are cold till you give them a whisper.

FAITH: But he'd never take a girl for a ride
down a road of deception.
And I love him for that.

TEASEL: You love him because he's faithful,
but pissed because he won't cheat.

FAITH: One day this will be you.

TEASEL: Me?!

FAITH: In love.

TEASEL: Nice try.
No way.
I'll never set myself up for the humiliation of love.
Not that I can't get a bit of action when I want it.
Slide up beside some sweet bit of flesh
and whisper softly in his ear:
"Would you look at your Mighty Miracle!
Wanna dip your stick in something sweet?"

FAITH: You're disgusting.

TEASEL: I'm hilarious.
They are quite silly though, aren't they.

FAITH: Men?

TEASEL: Their penises.
So squishy and nondescript when flaccid
and quite ridiculous when hard.

FAITH: You're terrible.

TEASEL: Like a big fat finger pointing at what it wants.

FAITH: You won't talk me out of love.

TEASEL: Even though you know it's hopeless?

FAITH: There's something there.
Between us.
I feel it.

TEASEL: Then let's go see him.

FAITH: Really?

TEASEL: Men are visual creatures.
If there's anything that will win his heart,
it's getting a glimpse of you.

Enter MOXY.

MOXY: Hey, ladies!!!

TEASEL: How goes it, Moxy?

MOXY: I could complain.

TEASEL: But we wouldn't want to hear it.

FAITH: How's your . . . Johnny?

MOXY: Screw my Johnny.

FAITH: Right, well, I just—
I haven't seen him for a while.

MOXY: Like I have?

FAITH: He's your husband.

MOXY: And all he wants to do is please me.

FAITH: Nothing wrong with that.

MOXY: Clearly no one's ever tried to please you.

FAITH: If I were married to a man like that,
I'd be curled in every night.

MOXY: Sounds like fun.

TEASEL: Don't you worry about him?

MOXY: Worry about what?

TEASEL: His wandering eye.

MOXY: He'd never.

TEASEL: Why not?

MOXY: He's a martyr.

TEASEL: So what?

MOXY: He gets off on persecution
and I give him plenty.

FAITH: You have one of the best husbands in the world.

MOXY: Best husbands! Ha!
A contradiction in terms.
If I were married to a bottle of tequila
I'd still find a reason to hate it.

FAITH: Ever consider Conscious Uncoupling?

MOXY: Now that sounds like a fascinating concept.

FAITH: I mean, as a process for completing a relationship in a loving way.

MOXY: That's such an appealing euphemism.

FAITH: Seriously, Conscious Uncoupling can be a catalyst for personal transformation because the grief of splitting up makes way for a personal breakthrough.

MOXY: Do you have any literature on the subject?

FAITH: I was just thinking . . . if you're so unhappy with him . . .

    RAZ enters.

RAZ: (*handing MOXY a sausage-on-a-stick*) Got you a sausage.

MOXY: Aw, thanks.
You guys know Raz?

TEASEL: Teasel.

FAITH: Faith.

RAZ: Cool.
(*to MOXY*) Careful, it's hot.

MOXY: Yowsers!

RAZ: Piping.

MOXY: See, girls, this is what new best friends are for.
Raz knows how much I love a nice hot sausage on a stick
so she goes and buys me a nice hot sausage on a stick.

RAZ: Yup.

MOXY: Raz doesn't even like hot sausage on a stick.

RAZ: More of a bun girl, myself.

MOXY: Hey, we should all do Nuit Blanche tonight!

RAZ: Yah.

MOXY: Get shit-faced and consume some corporate art!

TEASEL & FAITH: Uhhh . . .

MOXY: Come on. I'll guarantee hot sausages all 'round.

FAITH: I'm sort of on a cleanse.

MOXY: Come on, Faith. We gotta get you off the v-train.

FAITH: I'm not a virgin.

RAZ: No shame in that.
You're a gold star lesbian!

FAITH: I'm not a lesbian.

MOXY: She's just very fond of animals.

FAITH: I'm not a . . . I'm not a . . .

MOXY: Behhhhh (*sheep sound*)

TEASEL: Why don't we come around to your place
for drinks this afternoon.

MOXY: Can't promise my husband
and his fool won't be lurking around.

TEASEL: Fine by me.

FAITH: Yeah, yeah. Me too.

MOXY: Well, all right then.

RAZ: I'll catch up with you later.

TEASEL: Bye.

FAITH: Bye.

RAZ: Peace.

    TEASEL and RAZ exit.

MOXY: Hey, Faith.
(*handing her the sausage*) Finish this for me, will you.
I'm full.

FAITH: For the last time—I'm a vegan!

    FAITH stomps off.

MOXY: (*to audience*) It's good for her, you know.
Faith.
To get wound up and pissed off,
stamping her little feet,
puffing and pouting and looking for Teasel to save her
from my vicious attacks.
If I didn't do it, she'd float right out the window,
get swallowed up by her astrological sign.
It used to feel good to get her going.

And to whip words back and forth with Teasel,
but now there's something empty about it all.
Everything tastes the same.
Everything smells the same.
And everyone's trying so hard to be nice.

But no one is nice.
Everyone's just after their own happiness
even though happiness isn't a real emotion.

Fear—now there's an emotion.
You're running from a bear,
drowning in a river
standing at the edge of a cliff,
you feel it,
you can't help it.

Anger—there's another one.
Someone steals from you,
lies to you,
hurts someone you love,
you can't help but want to smash their face in.

Even sorrow is real.
Death . . . that'll get you there.

But happiness,
happiness is a cheat.
A poser.
An invention.
A name we've given to the absence
of any other emotion,
to the moments we're free of fear or anger or sorrow,
but that doesn't make happiness real.
In fact, it makes it nothing.

It's all bullshit, isn't it.
So we might as well have a little fun.

Music.

SCENE 2—THAT TEASEL IS . . .

CHARM: That Teasel is . . .

MIMI: Outrageous.

CHARM: Indeed!
I feel so . . . so . . .

MIMI: Furieux.

CHARM: Indeed!
And . . . and . . .

MIMI: Insulted and embarrassed and humiliated.

CHARM: And hot in the head
and clenched in the stomach
and hard in the—OH!!!
Mon dieu!

MIMI: Cousin?

CHARM: I know what's wrong with me.

MIMI: Cousin?

CHARM: Can it be?

MIMI: Cousin?

CHARM: I'm in love.

CHARM goes to his synthesizer.

MIMI films.

(spoken to the camera) You just, like, walked up to me, and, like, said things . . . lots of things . . . and I was just like . . . what? And then . . . I walked away . . . and I was like . . . oh.

HEART IN YOUR HAND

CHARM: *(sung)* You took my heart in your hand,
And squeezed with all your might.
You said, I could save myself,
But then you took a bite.
Now I'm a half-hearted man,
Looking back at you,
Trying to decide,
Just what I'm gonna do.

I really don't want to feel this way
When I listen to the things you have to say
But I do.
But I do.

You pulled my guts through my throat,
And threw them on the floor.
You said, I could follow you,
But then you slammed the door.
Now I'm a thin-gutted man,
Looking back at you.
Trying to decide,
What is really true.

I really don't want to feel this way
When I listen to the things you have to say
But I do.
But I do.

I really don't want to feel this way
But you are the predator,
I am the prey,
I love you.

Yes, I do.

MIMI: Bravo! Bravo!

CHARM: Look. Look!

MIMI: At what?

CHARM: My eyes.

MIMI: You have the real tears.

CHARM: Yes . . . yes, I do.
Mirror.

> *MIMI hands in the mirror.*

> *He looks with wonder at his tears.*

Tears.
There is a redness to my eyes.

MIMI: But it doesn't look bad.

CHARM: Quite the opposite.
It makes my irises blare with intensity.
Don't you think?

MIMI: Oh yes.

CHARM: Did you get it?

MIMI: Get it?

CHARM: The video?

MIMI: Ben oui.

CHARM: These are real tears.

MIMI: I know.

CHARM: I can't stop thinking about her.
But she's just so . . . mean.

MIMI: I think if it was me, wearing your shoes,
I would kidnap her in the park at night,
drag her back to my house,
strip her naked,
shut her up in a small, dark cupboard in the basement
and feed her only on the baguette and water
—maybe, occasionally, a glass of wine—
and never let her out until she knows
how a woman should act with a man.

CHARM: That's it.
Yes.
Mimi, yes.
Excellent idea.

MIMI: I will get the rope!

CHARM: I need to find a way to expose the way
she has exposed me
and maybe, in the process,
expose myself to elicit a sympathetic response
from her and/or my followers.

MIMI: Pardon?

CHARM: From now on, I will secretly record
every interaction I have with Teasel.
She will, no doubt, be as mean as she was just now
and I will show my reactions to her ruthless and unfounded criticisms
and when she sees the videos on my vlog of how cruel she has been,
she will apologize and love me for suffering with silent devotion.

MIMI: Silent?

CHARM: Well, not entirely silent.
I'll have to do a running commentary
to document my personal journey of pain and suffering.
I'll call it: Total Eclipse of the Heart.

MIMI: Merveilleux.

Music.

ACT 3

SCENE 1—WHAT IS THAT HEAVENLY SOUND?

FAITH and TEASEL have just arrived at MOXY and JOHNNY's condo.

MOXY: Wine or cosmo?

FAITH: Maybe I'll just go and say a quick hi to the guys.

MOXY: Or we could do Negronis?

FAITH: Nothing hard for me.

TEASEL: She's got a date.

FAITH: Teasel . . .

MOXY: Really? Who's the lucky dog?

FAITH: It's too soon to talk about.

MOXY: Balls, it is.

TEASEL: It's a secret.

MOXY: Then I wish my husband knew
because it wouldn't be a secret anymore.

TEASEL: Your husband can't keep a secret?

MOXY: He's not some straight-edge Christian, is he?

FAITH: No, no, I just—

MOXY: New-aged Buddhist?

FAITH: No, no—

MOXY: Muslim radical?

FAITH: What? No.

MOXY: Then have a drink with me.

FAITH: One drink.

MOXY: Yeah!!!!
Ladies!!!

> *Fills their glasses with a cocktail.*

To you, my dear friends.
May you one day be as blissfully married as I.

> *They drink.*

> *A horrible sound emanates from the other room.*

One minute.

> *MOXY exits to another room where HEARTFREE and JOHNNY are
> listening to records.*

What is that heavenly sound?

HEARTFREE: This band is virtually unheard of.

MOXY: Astonishing.

JOHNNY: If it's bothering you, we should talk about this.

HEARTFREE: I'm going to play it on my podcast.

MOXY: Podcast?

HEARTFREE: Yeah, it's sort of a new thing.

MOXY: What kind of a new thing?

HEARTFREE: It's like a podcast about music
from all places for all time.

MOXY: Inclusive.

JOHNNY: Don't waste your time, bro.

MOXY: That's not nice, Johnny.
I'm genuinely interested.

HEARTFREE: Well, it's sort of like I go through time and each
episode is—
each podcast is sort of an inner landscape of a—
well, the listening experience will be intersectional
and intercultural, of course, but each episode should ultimately
inspire some sort of visceral response.

MOXY: Visceral, yeah, I'm really getting that from this band.

HEARTFREE: Yeah?

MOXY: Yeah, like this music makes me feel sort of . . .
tortured, you know?

HEARTFREE: Yeah.

MOXY: And I don't know, sort of irritated, I guess?

HEARTFREE: Irritated?

MOXY: Yeah, like it's sort of grating on my nerves, sort of making me want to do something impulsive.

HEARTFREE: That's . . . good.

MOXY: Yeah?

HEARTFREE: You should follow your impulse.

MOXY: Yeah?

HEARTFREE: Express the way you're being provoked to feel.

MOXY: All right.

> *She breaks the record.*

> *JOHNNY and HEARTFREE make an audible sound of horror.*

JOHNNY: Moxy!

MOXY: Aw, sorry bro, I don't know what came over me.

JOHNNY: What are you doing?!

MOXY: Whoa, Johnny, temper!

JOHNNY: I'm not mad . . . just . . .

MOXY: What?

HEARTFREE: They only issued, like, fifty of these.

MOXY: Sorry, bro.
Maybe you should consider a trigger warning
for that podcast of yours.

JOHNNY: We should talk about this.

    MOXY smiles.

We need to talk about this.

    MOXY goes back to TEASEL and FAITH.

MOXY: Another.

FAITH: I'm still working on mine.

MOXY: Just a top-up then.

FAITH: I . . .

    MOXY pours the drink.

    MOXY gets a text.

MOXY: Ohhhh yeah!!!!
Raz scored some sweet-ass shit.
I gotta meet her now.

TEASEL: But we were just getting into it.

MOXY: Come with.

FAITH: I haven't finished my drink.

MOXY: Well, drink 'er down, girl.

TEASEL: You go. We'll meet you out.

MOXY: All right, I'll text.

TEASEL: Perfect.

MOXY: Later.

MOXY exits.

FAITH: You're amazing.

TEASEL: Don't thank me yet.

Enter JOHNNY and HEARTFREE.

JOHNNY: Sorry about that.

TEASEL: We all know what she's like.

HEARTFREE: Medusa and her venom.

FAITH: Maybe we should go.

JOHNNY: I'd rather you stay.

TEASEL: Sweet talking already!

JOHNNY: Sorry, I didn't mean to infer that I—

HEARTFREE: Maybe we should leave and let them get on with it.

FAITH: I . . .

JOHNNY: Can I get anyone a drink?

FAITH: (*indicating her drink*) I'm good for now.

JOHNNY: Oh, right, of course.

TEASEL: What sign are you, Johnny?

HEARTFREE: He's a Leo.

TEASEL: Interesting.
I wonder if Leos and Pisces go well together.
Faith?

FAITH: Teasel!

HEARTFREE: Are you into toothpicks, Faith?

JOHNNY: Heartfree!

TEASEL: Is Johnny a vegan, by any chance?

HEARTFREE: He's been flirting with it for years.
Allergic to beef, so that's a start.
And lactose intolerant.

TEASEL: Hey, Faith, he's halfway there.

FAITH: Okay. Enough.

HEARTFREE: You seem like quite the expert.

TEASEL: On vegans?

HEARTFREE: Relationships.

TEASEL: Only because I refuse to have them.

HEARTFREE: Sounds lonely.

TEASEL: Illuminating.
I can watch my friends fumble around
without getting chewed up and spit out myself.

JOHNNY: Sounds to me like you're scared of falling in love.

TEASEL: I would be, if there were any danger of it.

Knock at the door.

CHARM: *(from outside)* Jonathan? Heartfree?

HEARTFREE: Quiet, everyone. Don't let him know we're—

CHARM opens the door and walks in.

He is wearing a camera he thinks is well concealed.

CHARM: Hey there, bros.
Glad I caught you. It's been so long.

JOHNNY: Three days, at best.

CHARM: When you work as hard as I do,
a day can seem like a year.

HEARTFREE: Work?

CHARM: My status doesn't update itself.
Then there's the messages and the photos and the videos.
It really is very exhausting.

TEASEL: Yeah, it shows.

CHARM: Teasel!
Oh, I . . . I . . . please don't . . .
I really don't want to do this here.

TEASEL: What's wrong with you?

CHARM: Please.
These are my friends!

TEASEL: Are you okay?

CHARM: Have you no mercy!

JOHNNY: What's he talking about?

TEASEL: I have no idea.

CHARM: Typical . . . play the innocent,
when I'm sure you've already told them all about it.

TEASEL: About . . .

CHARM: Today.
At the park when you . . .
I can't repeat it.

TEASEL: Right.
I was simply asking Charm a few questions
about the artistic choices he chooses to make.

CHARM: Lies!
All lies.
She listed off about fifty of my faults

in less time than it would have taken me
to commit two of them.

HEARTFREE: What are they?

CHARM: My faults?

HEARTFREE: I'd love to know.
I always feel so inadequate next to you,
so hearing a fault or two might help me humanize you
and bolster my self-esteem.

CHARM: I'm sure Teasel would love to tell you herself
because she loves to humiliate people.

TEASEL: I don't know if I can remember.

CHARM: Well, she pretty much started at the top of my head
and worked her way down.
I think she said I should hold my hands like this,
am I right?
And my eyes, like this.
And my walk, there was something wrong with that too,
am I right?
How am I supposed to walk?
Maybe you can give us a demonstration
so all the men here know how we're supposed to move.
No?
Embarrassed, are you?
Shocked to hear how rude you were?
It was something like this, wasn't it?

*He walks about the room trying to highlight the absurdity of
TEASEL's criticism.*

Look at that cruel smirk.

HEARTFREE: Just saying, yo,
but for me, bro?
I'd be glad to find a girl who speaks her truth.

CHARM: Then look no further—bro.
I'm sure Teasel will give you an earful
of everything she thinks is wrong with you.

TEASEL: Thank you so much for the recommendation,
but I'd never sign up for a job
when I knew there'd be nothing to do.
With you, Charm, I know you'll always keep me busy.

CHARM: I told you she'd be rude.

HEARTFREE: I don't mind a bit of cheek,
as long as she follows her truth.

CHARM: *(aside)* Is he into her?
Is she into him?!
Miracles will never cease
if rude women and ignorant men
are capable of making a man of my quality,
my sincerity,
of my inner beauty, uneasy.

Well, friends, it's been real
but I'm afraid I have to fly.

JOHNNY: Already?

CHARM: I have eighteen coffee dates lined up for today.

HEARTFREE: Go easy on the caffeine, bro.

CHARM storms off.

You really wound him up.

TEASEL: And you sent him spinning!

HEARTFREE: So . . . I should go pick up my costume.

TEASEL: Costume?

HEARTFREE: Yeah, my friend's making this conceptual durational masquerade performance piece in the park for Nuit Blanche. You guys should come.

TEASEL: I'm not much of a performer.

HEARTFREE: It's not performing performing.
Like, you don't need any experience
and you don't need to know the concept,
and you don't really need to do anything,
just hang out and wear a disguise.

TEASEL: Maybe we can text you later. After . . . *(indicating FAITH and JOHNNY)*

HEARTFREE: Oh, right, yeah, cool.

TEASEL: *(to FAITH)* I'm heading out now, Faith.
You good?

FAITH: Oh yeah. Yeah.

HEARTFREE: Bye.

TEASEL exits.

HEARTFREE watches her go.

FAITH and JOHNNY look at one another.

HEARTFREE remembers he's supposed to leave too.

Oh!
Sorry.
Later, bro.

HEARTFREE exits.

FAITH: Alone.

JOHNNY: Yes.
Alone.

FAITH: Do you want to . . .

JOHNNY: Yes?

FAITH: Do you want . . .

JOHNNY: To play a board game?

FAITH: Always.

JOHNNY: Snakes and Ladders?

FAITH: Trouble?

JOHNNY: I've got Candy Land?

FAITH: I love Candy Land.

JOHNNY: Sweet.

He sets up the game.

What colour do you want to be?

FAITH: The colour of my beating heart.

JOHNNY: Red?

FAITH: I'm afraid it's green.

JOHNNY: Green?

FAITH: In jealous yearning over you.

JOHNNY: I guess that makes me blue.

FAITH: You don't have to be.

JOHNNY turns over a card.

JOHNNY: Red.

He moves.

FAITH: (*card*) Green.

JOHNNY: Why look at you.
Already up the Rainbow Trail.

FAITH: Guess I'm lucky that way.

JOHNNY: With rainbows?

FAITH: With getting what I want.

JOHNNY: (*card*) Orange.

FAITH: Do you forgive me?

JOHNNY: For what?

FAITH: Going after you.

JOHNNY: You have to be sorry to be forgiven.

FAITH: (*card*) Yellow.

JOHNNY: (*card*) Gingerbread Man.

FAITH: Look at you racing through the Peppermint Stick Forest.

JOHNNY: I'm still not as far as you.

FAITH: I can wait if I know you're coming.

JOHNNY: You know I'm a faithful guy.

FAITH: And that's what I love about you.

JOHNNY: And I wouldn't want to sacrifice what you love about me.

FAITH: But if your faithful heart is suffering,
doesn't it deserve a more deserving heart?

JOHNNY: How could you trust me if I was a cheat?

FAITH: I think I'd find a way.

JOHNNY: Go.

FAITH: I'm sorry?

JOHNNY: Your turn.

FAITH: Oh. (*card*) Purple.

JOHNNY: (*card*) Orange.

FAITH: (*card*) Peanut Brittle.
What if we just sat a little closer.

JOHNNY: I suppose that wouldn't hurt.

FAITH: And if you accidentally touched my leg.

JOHNNY: With my leg, you mean?

FAITH: Only because you're sitting a little closer.

JOHNNY: Then I suppose that wouldn't be wrong.

(*flipping a card*) I get to go through the Mountain Pass.

FAITH: (*aside*) I'll put him through my Mountain Pass!

(*flipping a card*) Red.
For me, this is all about choice.

JOHNNY: Choice?

FAITH: If we choose who we love, we're living to our greatest
potential.

JOHNNY: And Moxy and I chose one another.

FAITH: Yes, but then you got married.

JOHNNY: And marriage ruins love?

FAITH: There's no need to choose anymore,
so free-flowing honesty is chained to a train
barrelling on toward death.

JOHNNY: No exceptions?

FAITH: I would be one if you could marry me.

JOHNNY: Easy to say to a man chained to a train.

FAITH: Ever heard of monogam*ish*?

JOHNNY: (*card*) Ice Cream Float.

FAITH: Now look who's bounding ahead.
(*card*) Red.

JOHNNY: (*card*) Yellow.

FAITH: (*card*) Blue. Wait, I'm stuck.

JOHNNY: Until you draw another red.

FAITH: You're a treasure, Johnny.

JOHNNY: A treasure?

FAITH: A big chunk of bling
hanging round her neck.
And if I'm looking at her bling,
it's only because I'd know how to treat it right.

JOHNNY: Looking's not the problem.

FAITH: (*touching his leg*) Right, but I don't just want to look.
I want to feel it around my neck.
I want to polish it up and take it out
and show it around the town.
I want to keep it clean and shiny,
smell it slippery,

feel its weight,
and I'd be careful,
oh, so careful,
to bring it home at night.

> *She realizes he has a boner.*

> *He jumps up.*

JOHNNY: I'm sorry. I . . . I . . .

> *JOHNNY exits.*

FAITH: (*to audience*) I need a boyfriend.
And it's not because I'm weak.
Or dependent.
Or desperate.
I'm just so sick of doing things on my own.
Ordering takeout sushi,
ironically watching reality TV,
masturbating on the couch.

The down times are the worst:
the hour after I get home from work,
making coffee on Sunday mornings,
reading in bed before I turn off the light.
I've tried to fill the moments in between
with an incredible amount of activity,
but somehow the moments in between
manage to sneak back in.
And I can't lament my loneliness online
because the Internet is a sea of other peoples' triumphs,
other peoples' happiness,
other peoples' needs.

Dating sites are terrifying,
but I do it, I shop online.
And I try to approach it in the right way.
I just try to have fun,
and be my most confident self,
and brush off the losers,
and try not to care,
and try not to cling,
and try not to project too far into the future,
and if there were any other way to meet someone, I would,
but all my friends are hooked up,
all my friends are getting engaged,
all my friends are talking about weddings and houses and babies.

I know I shouldn't go for a married man.
What a ridiculous way to set myself up
for major disappointment,
but I can see it with him:
the winter.

Bundled in crocheted blankets
in an attic apartment
surrounded by obsolete recording equipment,
listening to records by candlelight,
drinking Pinot Noir and talking about the future.

We'll look out the window
and watch a snowstorm bury
our double-locked bikes down below.

My hands and feet get so cold in the winter.
I layer myself in wool, but the only thing that will do any good
is his body under the blankets.
He shrieks when I put my feet on his calf,

but he draws me into him
and holds me closer
and that's where I find myself
living whole and complete and full.
I can do anything with that kind of warmth.

Loneliness is unbearable in the snow.
I can't go another winter.

SCENE 2—EVERYBODY TITS OUT

Lights up on RAZ *rapping in a bar.*

RAZ: Ev'rybody tits out, dicks up,
Grindin' by the speakahs,
Twerkin' till dey hurtin'
in dey brand new sneakahs.
Flirtin' divertin'
Reapplying lipstick,
Sweatin' like an animal but gotta keep da hair slick.

Look at the virgin, tryna to get laid.
Look at the pusha-man, tryna to get paid.
Look at the bouncer, tired already.
Look at the bartender, tryna stay steady.

Yo, peep da jailbait out for da night,
Hangin' off the poser who's up for a fight.
Check out da intern tryin' not to throttle
His mutha-fucka lawyer friend who's buying by da bottle.

Dripping on the floor,
Fucking by the door,
Fingering a score,
Choking back the roar
Of self-doubt and hesitation:

(*more relaxed speaking*) What're you doing this for,
you stupid loser wannabe?
Look in the mirror and stop this shit
before you end up like your mum:
double jobbing, drinking hard,
screaming and slamming doors.
Stop this shit,
before you end up like your dad:
getting fat and yelling at the TV.
Stop this shit
before you end up like your sister:
knocked up in a suburb voting conservative
and reseeding brown patches on her lawn.
When you gonna stop this shit!
When you gonna stop this shit!

That's what they're thinking.
But not what they're doing.

Ev'rybody tits out, dicks up,
Grindin' by the speakahs,
Twerkin' till dey hurtin'
in dey brand new sneakahs.
Flirtin' divertin'
Reapplying lipstick,
Sweatin' like an animal but gotta keep da hair slick.[1]

 She bows and joins MOXY.

MOXY: Whooo!!!!!!

 They do a shot.

You smashed it, Raz! You smashed it up!

---

1 Writing contribution to "Everybody Tits Out" by Alicia Richardson.

RAZ: You're a savage lunatic.

MOXY: You're a beast without a cage.

RAZ: You're a bullshitter speaking her truth.

BOTH: Bitches wreaking havoc!!!

They do another shot.

RAZ: Oh shit.

MOXY: What?

RAZ: Some punk just walked in dressed in a giant penis costume.

MOXY: Stag party.

RAZ: No doubt.

MOXY: Do they pass that thing round?

RAZ: Must be covered in cum and disappointment.

MOXY: Dickheads.

RAZ: Dickheads.

MOXY: Dickheads!

RAZ: Cock-strutting with a shit-eating grin.

MOXY: "Who wants a penis selfie?!"

RAZ: "Honk if you like boners."

MOXY: "It's good luck if you high-five my foreskin."

RAZ: He totally high-fives.

MOXY: "Put 'er there."

They high-five one another in mockery.

Thinks he's brave.

RAZ: Thinks he's subversive.

MOXY: Thinks he's more than a cocky little shit.

RAZ: Let's go punch him in the face and push him off a bridge.

MOXY: Let's get his real cock out for comparison.

RAZ: Let's touch him where he says he wants to be touched.

MOXY: Let's get this shit started.

BOTH: Bitches wreaking havoc!!!

A blast of music.
The chaos of Nuit Blanche.
MOXY and RAZ exit.
Honking cars, loud music, people yelling.

A man in a penis costume runs on.
He's running for his life.
He trips and looks back in terror at his unseen assailants.

Black out.
Intermission.

ACT 4

SCENE 1—SUCH A GREAT PERK

JOHNNY and HEARTFREE are making candles.

JOHNNY: Such a great perk.

HEARTFREE: Right?

JOHNNY: Twenty bucks for a homemade candle.
Who wouldn't donate?

HEARTFREE: Thanks for helping.

JOHNNY: How much will you make?

HEARTFREE: Huh?

JOHNNY: For the podcast?

HEARTFREE: Well, the organic beeswax and organic scented oils
were a bit more than I thought they would be.

JOHNNY: Sure, but you can't compromise your—

HEARTFREE: Exactly, and because candles are fragile,
I had to order these special boxes
made from recycled toilet paper rolls.

JOHNNY: Right, so after postage, what?
You'll make ten bucks per donation?

HEARTFREE: Well . . .

JOHNNY: Eight?

HEARTFREE: More like . . .

JOHNNY: Five?

HEARTFREE: I'll probably clear about two,
but this whole thing's more about publicity anyway.

JOHNNY: Totally.

HEARTFREE: Totally.

> *JOHNNY's phone dings.*
> *He looks at it and shakes his head.*

What is it?

JOHNNY: A selfie of Moxy with a stagette party.

HEARTFREE: They don't know what they're in for.

JOHNNY: She likes to send me before and after shots.

HEARTFREE: Why?

JOHNNY: She knows it gets to me.

HEARTFREE: You really don't need this, bro.

JOHNNY: I just wish she'd talk to me.

HEARTFREE: Women can be jerks.

JOHNNY: I can't do anything if she doesn't talk to me.

HEARTFREE: But can you imagine a world without them?

JOHNNY: I'm paralyzed.

HEARTFREE: Guess I wouldn't have to look this good.

JOHNNY: You'd still be trying to look that good
to look better than other men.

HEARTFREE: Looking good's about trying to catch a lady.
Without them, I'd peel myself out of these skinny jeans.

JOHNNY: I'd shave my beard.

HEARTFREE: I'd comb my hair.

JOHNNY: No more tattoo-planning coffee dates.

HEARTFREE: No more riding bikes to farmers' markets.

JOHNNY: No more Midsummer's-eve-axe-throwing.

HEARTFREE: No more singer/songwriters
in tiny little bars.

> Both laugh.

JOHNNY: I always grab a table near the front.

HEARTFREE: You're trying to be seen.

JOHNNY: Or what's the point?

HEARTFREE: The music.

JOHNNY: Oh, I'm listening to the music
but I'm also listening to the women,
circled at tables nearby.

HEARTFREE: And then?

JOHNNY: I make sure I'm looking very still and serious.

HEARTFREE: Because you're listening to the music.

JOHNNY: Right, I'm listening to the music
but it's just as important to be seen to be listening to the music
as it is to listen to the music.

HEARTFREE: Well, music's my thing, so—

JOHNNY: Then I wait.

HEARTFREE: For what?

JOHNNY: The singer/songwriter to tell a joke in between her songs.
And then I laugh.

HEARTFREE: Right.

JOHNNY: In a contained but audible kind of way.
I scratch my beard.
I sip my IPA
and watch the women watch
what I'm going to do next.

HEARTFREE: And what if there aren't any jokes?

JOHNNY: If the music's good, I keep staring intensely.

HEARTFREE: And if not?

JOHNNY: Then I lean in to talk to my buddy.
We chat.
And in that conversation
I attempt to cycle through all of my expressions:
sympathy, care, humour,
demonstrating every form of communication
I'm capable of.

HEARTFREE: That's what you're up to.

JOHNNY: Come on. You know.

HEARTFREE: I know?

JOHNNY: I know you know.

HEARTFREE: I know you know I know you know.

Both laugh.

JOHNNY: Do you ever . . .

HEARTFREE: What?

JOHNNY: Practise?

HEARTFREE: What?

JOHNNY: Your facial expressions.

HEARTFREE: Right.

JOHNNY: In the mirror.

HEARTFREE: Do you?

JOHNNY: Heck yeah!

HEARTFREE: Me too.
How to talk.

JOHNNY: And how to listen.

HEARTFREE: I gotta say, I'm pretty good.

JOHNNY: I know you are.

HEARTFREE: I'm really good,
but there's one expression I can never figure out.

JOHNNY: Which one?

HEARTFREE: You know, you're in a bar
and there's a powerful woman
with a powerful voice
singing a powerful song.

JOHNNY: Yeah.

HEARTFREE: And it's the kind of song that starts
taking men to task for,
well, everything.

JOHNNY: Like sexual harassment?

HEARTFREE: Or rape and spousal abuse.

JOHNNY: Or the proliferation of war, capitalism, and the annihilation of the planet?

HEARTFREE: Yes, and the song is justifiable.

JOHNNY: Yes, it's a defensible position.

HEARTFREE: Men have been shit.

JOHNNY: Men have been shit.

HEARTFREE: But I'm not.

JOHNNY: Check your privilege.

HEARTFREE: Well, I'm trying not to be.

JOHNNY: Check your privilege, bro.

HEARTFREE: And the women, they're hooting and hollering
and cheering the singer/songwriter on with a vengeance,
with a look of blood and desire and rage
and they're laughing at the song,
at the pointed irony
and they're looking at the men in the room
to see how they will react.

JOHNNY: I'm starting to see your problem.

HEARTFREE: If I laugh along,
it's like I'm appropriating their oppression.
Like I'm saying I understand what it's like
not to be a straight, white, cisgender, able-bodied man.

JOHNNY: Privilege checked.

HEARTFREE: And not only do I understand,
but I feel justified in participating
in the modicum of joy women get
from enacting some sort of cathartic, artistic revenge.

JOHNNY: And if you don't laugh along?

HEARTFREE: Even worse.
Then I somehow ally myself with the man of the past,
the man who wants to go on perpetrating
crimes against women, children, and humanity at large.

JOHNNY: So, what do you do when someone sings a song like that?

HEARTFREE: I blow my nose.

JOHNNY: Then you must be blowing your nose
for half the show.

HEARTFREE: Half the time, yeah.

JOHNNY: And no girl wants to make out
with a bro who has the flu.

HEARTFREE: Or allergies.

JOHNNY: Yeah, I mean, what if she has a cat?

HEARTFREE: Or a ferret.

JOHNNY: Right, and she's watching you sneeze thinking:
I'd love to bring that guy home,
but he'd be allergic to my guinea pig.

HEARTFREE: It's hard to be a nice guy.

JOHNNY: There's just no precedent.

HEARTFREE: I try to rely on honesty, but it's more complicated than it seems.

JOHNNY: Honestly.

Beat.

HEARTFREE: So . . . did you finally let Faith through the walls of your fortress?

JOHNNY: She was pounding at the gate.
Had my soldier at attention.

HEARTFREE: Bro!

JOHNNY: My forces won't hold up much longer.

HEARTFREE: Then the sooner you surrender, the better.

JOHNNY: Is that what you're going to do?

HEARTFREE: Me?

JOHNNY: Teasel's into you.

HEARTFREE: What? No.
I mean I totally love her for the way she bats
at buddy down the hall.

JOHNNY: You could go for it
and see how it plays out.

HEARTFREE: Yeah, but is that what she wants?
Is that what I want?
You know, I find it really hard to know what I want.

JOHNNY: What do you mean?

HEARTFREE: Like so many times a day I think:
that's what I want.
And I can see whatever it is—
a job, a woman, a macchiato—
sitting there, just out of reach.
But in the process of stretching out my hand to get it,
I start to doubt myself:
Is that what I want?
What I really really want?
And if I choose that thing,
if I make a decision to go for it,
will I close myself off to other opportunities?
So, then I think:
maybe I should wait and think about it again
to make sure I'm making the right choice.
You know?

JOHNNY: Yeah, I know.

JOHNNY embraces HEARTFREE.

HEARTFREE: Guess we should get in our costumes.

JOHNNY: Don't know if I feel like it.

HEARTFREE: It's Nuit Blanche.

JOHNNY: Yeah.

HEARTFREE: And Teasel and Faith are going to meet us there.

JOHNNY: Really?

HEARTFREE: Or you could spend all night staring at texts from your wife.

JOHNNY: Let's do this.

> *Both laugh . . . as if.*
> *Music.*

SCENE 2—IS HE DEAD? DID WE KILL HIM?

> *RAZ and MOXY run on.*

RAZ: *Is* he dead? Did we kill him?

MOXY: No, I heard him groaning.

RAZ: Then what was that stink?

MOXY: Regret.

RAZ: Regret?

MOXY: For being a dickhead.

RAZ: Nothing worse than dickhead drama.

MOXY: The fountain was genius.

RAZ: Shivering, poor thing,
with the penis costume up over his head,
skinny jeans around his ankles,

his little wormy wiggling all about
as he squirmed and shrieked and fought to get free.

MOXY: No wonder the stagette party pranced in.

RAZ: You think she recognized her groom-to-be
by his trembling little wiggly?

MOXY: That, or by his curdling screams.

RAZ: Yo, she never would have heard them
over her own shrieking and swearing
and rushing to cover him up
with that rat-tail of dollar-store lingerie.

MIMI enters carrying CHARM's dry cleaning.

MOXY: Now, what do we have here?

RAZ: This is the cousin I was telling you about.

MIMI: Oh, Raz. Bonsoir.

MOXY: Well, enchanter.

RAZ: Moxy, Mimi. Mimi, Moxy.

MIMI: Enchanter, but you must excuse me.
I need to deliver this dry cleaning to my cousin.

RAZ: At this time of night?

MIMI: There is a very convenient twenty-four-hour service.

RAZ: Yeah, that's cool,
I just think you should take some time
to go off the clock.

MIMI: And just what would I do if I got off on this clock.

RAZ: I can think of one or two things that might tick your tock.

MOXY: (*grabbing the dry cleaning*) Let's see what we've got here.

MIMI: Oh, please. I cannot expose the fabric to the night air.

RAZ: (*grabbing MIMI*) Can I expose you to the night air?

MIMI: Ooo la la.

> MOXY *rips off the plastic and starts to get dressed in* CHARM's *clothes.*

Oh no no no no.
Please.
Charm will feel the emotions.

RAZ: And what about your emotions?

MIMI: Pardon?

RAZ: Don't your emotions need feeling?

MIMI: My emotions?

RAZ: You're wasting all your freedom
playing servant to a fool.

MIMI: Oh, Charm is not a fool.

RAZ: Many would beg to differ.

MIMI: Then they do not know him like I know him.

RAZ: And how exactly do you know him?

MIMI: As a beautiful, vulnerable soul
reaching out to touch the world
with his intense and honest music.

RAZ: Well, I think you should hang with us tonight.

MIMI: What are you planning to do?

RAZ: We never plan to do anything.
But the world's pretty good at throwing things our way.

MIMI: And am I one of those things?

RAZ: Do you want to be?

MOXY is dressed in CHARM's clothes and looks like a guy.

MOXY: What do you think?

RAZ: Yeahhhh.

MIMI: Oh la la.

MOXY: Do I look it?

RAZ: Bro, you look it.

MOXY: *(mimicking a man)* Brooooo!!!!
What up, broooo!!!

Just gotta adjust my balls.
My balls get sweaty.
Ball sweat.
I get it.
All.
The.
Time.
Ball sweat like glue sticking my balls to my thighs.
Oh, man, do I need some talc.
Oh, man, do I need some porn.

She pulls out her phone and pretends to watch porn.

Oh yeah . . .
Porn . . .

Pretending to masturbate like a man.

Oh yeah . . .
Titties, oh yeah . . .

(as herself) How's that?

RAZ: You need a more faraway look.

MOXY: Like this?
(trying again) Oh yeah . . . porn.

RAZ: Kinda, yeah, like you're watching porn,
but also kinda looking through it at the same time,
looking deep in and past the sex
to some faraway rainbow land,
or maybe just deep and into yourself,
transported to the blissful nothingness
of going for the cum.

RAZ pulls out her phone and pretends to watch porn and mas-turbate like a man.

Like this:
(*trying*) Oh yeah . . . fake lesbians making out . . . hawwttt!

MOXY: Oh right, right.

MIMI: Non non non,
you've both got it wrong.
First you need to coax up the boner.
Like this:
"Allez . . . allez . . . allez, Monsieur Pénis!"

All three pretend to masturbate like men.

Loud music.

SCENE 3—WELCOME TO ALL MUSIC FROM ALL PLACES FOR ALL TIME

Lights up on HEARTFREE recording his first podcast.

HEARTFREE: Welcome to All Music from All Places for All Time.
A podcast about listening
and feeling
and responding in a visceral,
well, not necessarily in a visceral—
well, in some way,
hopefully.
Okay, so this first podcast is called: From the Cave.
So you think of cavemen and cavewomen
and you think of . . . what?
Banging rocks together,
drawing on walls,

building fires.
Well, rather than leaning on assumptions
and jumping to conclusions about what music
they may or may not have made,
I've tried to immerse myself in the world of the caveman—
to approach it from the inside,
sort of like those method actors, maybe,
but I'm not trying to be a caveman,
just to simulate the lived experience of a . . .
in order to curate music that . . .

Well, for example,
to prepare myself for this episode,
I've been eating Paleo,
hanging out with the rewilding community,
going wild-water collecting,
and foraging for edible mushrooms.

> *Lights slowly rise on* TEASEL *dressed as a badly taxidermied fox.*
> *She is in the park listening to* HEARTFREE's *podcast.*

I've been challenging domestication,
trying to live seasonally
and while I'm doing this,
I'm listening.
Listening to the sounds around me, yes,
but also listening to my breath,
to my heartbeat as I eat raw meat,
and fingerpaint in the old quarry,
gathering internal information,
and I've let those sounds,
those experiences
inform the music I've curated for the podcast.

Today you're gonna hear a bit of microtonal,
a bit of co-improvisational,
a bit of invented instrument-driven music,
maybe even a little Phil Collins.
Just kidding.
Imagine?

So sit back,
turn down the lights,
find your cave,
and enjoy.

Music.

SCENE 4—WHAT ARE YOU LISTENING TO?

Lights remain up on TEASEL *in the park.*
FAITH enters dressed as an angel.

FAITH: What are you listening to?

TEASEL: Oh, nothing. I mean . . . just a podcast.

FAITH: Which one?

TEASEL: It's a new one I'm—
It's a friend who . . .
Hey, do me a favour and finish stuffing my back.

FAITH: No one's going to get it.

TEASEL: I was stuffed by an amateur.

FAITH: You told me, yeah.

TEASEL: He used pipe cleaners for bones.

FAITH: Right.

TEASEL: He bent the joints the wrong way.

FAITH: Sure.

TEASEL: I'm a meme.

FAITH: No one's going to get
that you're dressed up as a badly taxidermied fox.

TEASEL: Yeah? And what are you, a Q-tip?

FAITH: I'm an angel.

TEASEL: Well, let's go see if we can find them
so we don't have to stand here feeling awkward all night.

> *They exit.*
> *CHARM enters dressed as Daphne in the process of becoming a tree.*
> *He tries to subtly follow FAITH and TEASEL.*
> *MIMI hurries on.*

CHARM: Where have you been?

MIMI: Oh . . . I was just . . . doing some location scouting
for your next video.

CHARM: *(handing her a raccoon hat and squirrel gloves)* Well, put
these on.
We need to stay hidden,
which is why I've cunningly disguised myself
as Daphne in the process of transformation.

Oh, my heart.

MIMI: Cousin?

CHARM: It's ripping a hole in my chest.
Beat by beat it thumps with fear and jealousy.

MIMI: Are you certain they are planning a rendezvous, ici?

CHARM: That, Mimi, is one of my many talents.
I sense . . . everything.

MIMI: Oh, cousin.

CHARM: I also saw them making plans online.
Oh, that floppy flirt, Heartfree.
I don't buy his goofy-grinned innocence for a moment.
The minute Teasel becomes vulnerable,
he will stomp all over her.

MIMI: Should we poison him and drop him down a well?

CHARM: Maybe.

MIMI: Chain him to a pickup truck and drag him through the streets?

CHARM: Perhaps.

MIMI: Douse him in gasoline and throw matches at him?

CHARM: A definite possibility, but for now get the camera rolling.

FAITH *and* TEASEL *enter again.*

Quick! Hide in my branches.

MIMI hides behind CHARM, which makes it look like there is a raccoon and two squirrels perched on the tree branches.

TEASEL: So the concept of this dance piece is that we stand here looking bored?

FAITH: It's called: My Version of a Performance of a Party Waiting to Happen.

TEASEL: Maybe we should just go to a bar.

Enter JOHNNY and HEARTFREE dressed as 1960s Batman and Robin.

Just keep walking. Keep walking.

FAITH: What?

TEASEL: Ironic superheroes at twelve o'clock.

FAITH: Oh no.

TEASEL: Why do I let you talk me into this shit. Pretend to fix my stuffing. Maybe they won't see us.

CHARM pops his head out.

CHARM: There he is!

MIMI: Sacre bleu!

CHARM: I can tell by his well-formed thighs and perfectly proportioned torso.

MIMI: Everyone looks good in coloured tights.

CHARM inches forward throughout this next scene.

JOHNNY: Hey, Robin?

HEARTFREE: Yes, Batman?

JOHNNY: Do you see those damsels in distress?

HEARTFREE: All I see is a badly taxidermied fox.

TEASEL: See!

HEARTFREE: And a toilet bowl cleaner.

FAITH: I'm an angel!

JOHNNY: If you examine them closely, Robin,
you'll see they're in disguise.

HEARTFREE: Holy camouflaged bombshells, Batman,
you're right!

JOHNNY: You ladies haven't been harassed by any supervillains,
have you?

TEASEL: Just by a couple of losers in spandex.

JOHNNY: Whammo!

HEARTFREE: Did you hear that, Batman?

JOHNNY: Sure did, Robin.

HEARTFREE: We'd better get that chip off her shoulder
before she succumbs to the weight of it
and sinks into the earth's crust.

JOHNNY: Precisely, Robin.
Good instinct.
But we're not equipped for that tonight.

TEASEL: Don't seem to be equipped for much,
if you ask me.

Enter MOXY and RAZ.

HEARTFREE: Red alert, Batman.

JOHNNY: Holy bad situation, Robin.
Let's put the evacuation plan in play.

They casually try to sneak off.

MIMI: (*seeing RAZ*) Mon coeur!

CHARM: Shhh.

MOXY: Well, what have we here?

RAZ: Looks like a badly taxidermied fox and a tampon to me.

TEASEL: Hah!

RAZ: You need some blood to finish the look.

FAITH: I'm an angel.

MOXY: And here I thought you had a date.

FAITH: No . . . I mean I did . . . but . . . it's over . . .

MOXY: So you thought you'd play dress-up.
Kinky.

TEASEL: We were just heading out.

MOXY: Leaving your superheroes behind?

TEASEL: They're not ours.

MOXY: Hey, Underoos and cheeky cheeks!
Where are you flying off to in such a hurry?

They shrug.

Strong quiet types.
At least they're showing what they're selling.
Am I right?

RAZ: So right.

MOXY: Especially this one.
Such a taut little bum.
You ladies mind if I pinch his weenie?

TEASEL: Do we have to have another conversation about consent?

The men dodge MOXY.

MOXY: Wouldn't mind a pint of prick is all.
Sober me up.
Been on the hunt for trouble,
but it's just so hard to get some release.

TEASEL: You're a wild woman, Moxy.

MOXY: Feral, even.
I mean it's impossible to know what I'll do next.

She slaps the JOHNNY's ass.

RAZ cracks up.

Let's get this party started.

RAZ: Where to next?

MOXY: We could throw lighters at the flame throwers?
Or try to pop one of those giant balloons.
Get high and do some rooftop parkour.

JOHNNY: Don't do that.

MOXY: Oh relax, Batman, you sound just like my husband.
"Do this, don't do that, you're going to get yourself arrested or seriously maimed."

JOHNNY: Maybe he's just trying to protect you.

MOXY: Maybe I don't need his protection.

JOHNNY: Maybe he understands that your desire for self-sabotage is a manifestation of your insecurity and low self-worth.

MOXY: Maybe my husband's been reading too many self-help books.

JOHNNY: Maybe he cares about you.

MOXY: Maybe he "cares" about everyone.

JOHNNY: Maybe he thinks of caring for people as a responsible way to be a citizen in this world.

MOXY: Do you do tricks, Batman?

JOHNNY: What?

MOXY: Flex your muscles,
throw boomerangs,
jump from windows, that kind of thing.

JOHNNY: I don't know what you're—

MOXY: Come on, you gotta do something to impress the tampon.

> *Beat.*

Have fun kids.
And don't keep him out too late.
He has tai chi in the morning with a bunch of old ladies.

> *RAZ and MOXY leave.*

CHARM: (*to MIMI*) Moxy's wearing some fabulous jeans.

MIMI: Oh, really?
I didn't notice.

CHARM: We should get me a pair like that.

> *The boys take off their masks.*

FAITH: It's Johnny!

TEASEL: Seriously?

> *It's been obvious for a while.*

FAITH: Do you think Moxy knew it was him?

TEASEL: Oh, Faith.

JOHNNY: I'm sorry about that.

TEASEL: It's not your fault.

HEARTFREE: She can't have a good time if anyone else is.

JOHNNY: And now our night is ruined.

TEASEL: Our night is just beginning.

FAITH: Let me buy you a hot chocolate?

JOHNNY: Okay. Yeah. Sure.

    FAITH and JOHNNY exit.

CHARM: Now they're alone!
Let's get closer, so we can hear what they say.
Keep filming!

HEARTFREE: The superhero thing was Johnny's idea.

TEASEL: It's cool.

HEARTFREE: Liar.

TEASEL: You're just not the type of guy who needs a mask.

HEARTFREE: Yeah, I'm pretty cute.

TEASEL: It's the curls.

    Beat.

I listened to your podcast.

HEARTFREE: Really?

TEASEL: Yeah.

HEARTFREE: I mean, I sort of think about it as still in the prototype phase.
I mean, as I go on, I think it'll—

TEASEL: I liked it.

HEARTFREE: Oh . . . really?

TEASEL: The way you're thinking about music through a multi-disciplinary, experiential framework creates the groundwork for an auditory intersectionality to naturally reveal itself.

HEARTFREE: Yeah . . . exactly.

TEASEL: And it's fascinating, the way you're interrogating the form itself by truly entering the "pod" before broadcasting.

HEARTFREE: You got that—good.

TEASEL: And exposing the mechanics of your process implicates the listener in the curation process and provokes them to participate in the internalization of the music.

HEARTFREE: Really?

TEASEL: I just wanted to sit still in the dark and listen.

HEARTFREE: Well, maybe you should come over some time and we can listen to some music.
I've got a huge record collection.

TEASEL: Yeah?

HEARTFREE: Yeah.

TEASEL: Yeah?

HEARTFREE: Yeah.

Ah. Like . . . lots.

> *They are about to kiss.*
> *CHARM makes sounds to stop them:*
> *Raccoon hiss, cat screech, dog bark, owl hoot.*
> *TEASEL and HEARTFREE look around.*

Wanna check out the giant robotic baby?

TEASEL: All right.

HEARTFREE: Cool.

TEASEL: Cool.

> *They exit.*

CHARM: (*turning toward the camera*) "Behold! Even nature cannot bear to—
(*remembering his video persona*) watch these haters, like, break my heart. Let's see, like, what they'll do next . . ."

> *FAITH and JOHNNY return sipping hot chocolate.*
> *CHARM and MIMI are stuck hiding.*

FAITH: I'm really sorry.

JOHNNY: For what?

FAITH: For putting you in an awkward position.

JOHNNY: That's not your fault.

FAITH: But I feel bad
because I can't help myself.

JOHNNY: You're not the only one who's being tempted here.

FAITH: But I'm the bad guy.

JOHNNY: Hey, no you're not.

FAITH: I keep pushing you to do
what you don't want to do.

JOHNNY: It's not that I don't want to do
what you'd like me to do.

FAITH: Really?

JOHNNY: Which makes me the bad guy.

FAITH: You couldn't be a bad guy if you tried.

JOHNNY: But I'm a jerk.

FAITH: You're not a jerk.
You're the kindest person I know;
I'm the jerk.

JOHNNY: You're not the jerk,
you're amazing.

FAITH: I don't feel amazing right now.

JOHNNY: You're lovely and sweet and beautiful.

FAITH: Beautiful?

JOHNNY: Well, I'm primarily attracted to your strength and intelligence and undeniable wisdom, but your beauty is also . . .

FAITH: Yes?

JOHNNY: I'm sorry, I'm an asshole.

FAITH: I'm the asshole.

JOHNNY: Well, I'm the bigger asshole.

FAITH: I'm clearly the biggest asshole in this situation.

JOHNNY: Don't say that.

FAITH: But it's true because I simply can't hide the fact that I'm in love with you.

JOHNNY: You are?

FAITH: I'm sorry if that's too much
but it's burning me up
and there's nothing I can do
to stop this flame from spreading.

    Beat.

JOHNNY: Then let it spread.

FAITH: Really?

JOHNNY: Let it melt us both.

FAITH: So I can . . . touch you?

    She takes his hand.

MIMI approaches while filming.

JOHNNY: Wait a minute,
over here.

He leads her to CHARM's tree.

FAITH: You're so beautiful.

JOHNNY: I still don't know if I can—
don't know if I want—

FAITH: You do.

JOHNNY: I do?

FAITH leans in to kiss Johnny.

MIMI: Vive l'amour!

FAITH and JOHNNY look at her.
CHARM and MIMI run away
Music.

ACT 5

DANCE PIECE: GOTTA GET HOME WITHOUT BEING SEEN.

- *running*
- *hiding*
- *holding hands while running and hiding*
- *pulling off costume pieces*
- *helping one another pull off costume pieces*

SCENE 1—DID YOU FOLLOW THEM?

CHARM is trying to get out of his costume.
MIMI enters out of breath.

CHARM: Did you follow them?

MIMI: Oui, oui.

CHARM: And where did they lead you?

MIMI: Right here.

CHARM: Down the hall?

MIMI: Chez eux.

CHARM: All four of them?

MIMI: Tous ensemble.

CHARM: The cheek!
They're probably up to their elbows in orgy as we speak.
Ohhhhh!!!
My heart can't bear the thought.
I'm suffocating in sorrow.

MIMI: Should we go make an interruption?

CHARM: And give them the chance to humiliate me,
kick me out,
and get back to their illicit act with scornful pleasure.

MIMI: Do you want me to film your despair?

CHARM: No, Mimi, no!
Don't you see I need a break from the spotlight?

MIMI: Pardon. I didn't mean to—

CHARM: Besides, I have a better idea.

MIMI: But, of course.

CHARM: Moxy!

MIMI: I think Moxy is still making the party with Raz.

CHARM: But she won't be for long
when you send her the video.

MIMI: Which video?

CHARM: Of Faith and Johnny caught in the illicit act.

MIMI: But they did not kiss.

CHARM: Oh, Mimi Mimi Mimi Mimi,
you're so innocent.
It's one of the many things I adore about you.
Now, *I* know they didn't kiss.

MIMI: Oui.

CHARM: And you know they didn't kiss.

MIMI: Oui.

CHARM: But if you didn't know what we know
when you were looking at the very end of that video,
what would you think?

MIMI: I would think that they kiss?

CHARM: Precisely.

MIMI: So . . . you want me to lie to Moxy?

CHARM: No, Mimi Mimi Mimi Mimi, not lie, no.
Just pre-empt the truth.

MIMI: Ahhhh.
Pardon?

CHARM: We both know what they are up to right now.
And Lord knows their promiscuous energy
has rubbed off on Heartfree and . . . Teasel.
But it is our responsibility,
nay, it's our duty,
to expose the betrayal of honest lovers
—like me and Moxy—
by sneaky, lascivious, demonic creatures
like the rest of them.

MIMI: Oh, je comprend: the hands justify the means.

CHARM: Then what are you waiting for?

MIMI: I wonder, perhaps, if it will be better
if I deliver this message on person.

CHARM: Why?

MIMI: Maybe Moxy will not look at the message.
Maybe she will not be recognizing them.
Maybe she will be angry with me.
If I go on person,
I can make certain she understand the circumstance is serious.

CHARM: And bring her back here.

MIMI: Exactement!

CHARM: Parfait!
And meanwhile, I will don a disguise,
infiltrate their lair, and make sure nothing happens.

MIMI: We will make them all suffer and beg for mercy.

CHARM: Yes.

MIMI: We will make them writhe in excruciating pain!

CHARM: Well . . .

MIMI: We will make them beg for a quick death while we—

CHARM: Mimi!

MIMI: Oui?

CHARM: Go!

Music.

SCENE 2—HEY EVERYONE

MOXY with a microphone at a wedding she's crashed.
She's still in drag.

MOXY: Hey, everyone.
If I could just have your attention for a minute.
I know the speeches have come and gone,
but at a wedding, call me crazy,
I think you can never have too many speeches.

I just have to say a few words about my buddy Jason here.
Jasooooon!!!
Now he's pretending he doesn't know me,
because he knows exactly what I'm going to say.
I'm gonna say it, Jason.
I'm gonna say it.

Rippers!!!
Crack cocaine!!!
Gay sex!!!
You name it, Jason's done it.

I got hitched, myself, a year ago today—
woo-hoo!!!!—
and I am telling you guys,
you are in for one hell of a treat.
If you think you're happy now!
If you think it couldn't get any better than this!
If you think you couldn't possibly be more defined by your
cisgender, just wait until other married people
start looking to you to commiserate:

"Is your wife as big a nag as my wife?"
"Is your husband as incompetent as my husband?"

But what else are you going to do?
Oh, come on, Jason and . . . new wife of Jason
. . . you know what I mean.
You guys have clearly "settled" for each other
But, realistically, what's the alternative.

Keep living the single life?
    —Cool, until your friends all couple off and don't want to go
    out anymore.
Polyamory?
    —Sooo cool but sooo many conversations.
Devoting yourself to a fascinating, well-paid, socially conscious,
all-consuming occupation?
    —Tell me if you find one of those lying around.
Or I guess you could just—be alone.

All things considered, Jason and . . .
(*looks in audience for name*) Michaela, you've done the thing that
most people do
and I am so impressed that it looks like you're able
to think of that as a triumph.

To Jason and Michaela!

SCENE 3—MY PLACE IS JUST AROUND THE CORNER

    *MIMI and RAZ making out at the back of the room at the wed-
    ding reception.*

RAZ: My place is just around the corner.

MIMI: Ohhhh.

RAZ: Let's get out of here, my little poutine.

MIMI: Ohhhh.

RAZ: Then I can really get your gravy flowing.

MIMI: Oh, oui oui oui
but . . .

RAZ: No . . . no buts.
Unless it's yours on my futon.

MIMI: Charm is depending on me.

RAZ: Screw Charm.

MIMI: He is counting on me to show the video to Moxy.

RAZ: What's the big deal about the video—
they could be, I don't know, wrestling or something.

MIMI: What I saw was not wrestling or something.

RAZ: And what did you see.

MIMI plays FAITH, RAZ plays JOHNNY.

MIMI: The lover say the soft thing.
And then the man, he looks upon the ground.
The lover, she take him by the hand;
he turn his head the other way.
Then she squeeze very hard;
then he pull away softly.
Then she take him in her arms;
then he give her a little pat.
Then she kiss his neck,

then he say, no . . . no . . .
Then she tremble;
then he sigh;
tremble;
sigh
tremble
sigh.
Then she grow bold,
then he grow weak.
She throw him down
and start to make the mad, passionate love with him.

    RAZ is into the make-out.

Raz . . .

RAZ: Oui?

MIMI: Do you love me?

RAZ: Oui.

MIMI: Then you will do whatever I ask of you?

RAZ: Oui, oui, oui.

MIMI: I want you to tell Moxy everything I told you.

RAZ: Mischief!

MIMI: Then I'm sure we can get her into an Uber.

RAZ: I told you, I'm not into gossip
or pushing people along a road of self-realization.

MIMI: Don't you think she'll want to know?

RAZ: Sure, but the messenger always gets shot.

MIMI: Not if there are two.
Don't make me do this alone.
We will show her the video,
drag her back to her condo,
and by the time we get there,
I will be so hot and sweaty
and looking for a place to put my madness.

RAZ: You sure you just don't want to go back to mine?

MIMI: Oh Moxy! Raz has something she want to show you.

Music.

SCENE 4—YOU'VE GOT TO ADMIRE HER ENERGY

MOXY and JOHNNY's condo.
JOHNNY, TEASEL, HEARTFREE, and FAITH are grouped around
JOHNNY's phone.
All of them are half-dressed.

TEASEL: You've got to admire her energy.

FAITH: Is she streaking a wedding reception?

HEARTFREE: I didn't know she was going to a wedding.

TEASEL: I'm sure she wasn't until she saw the open bar.

JOHNNY: Moxy won't be home any time soon.

HEARTFREE: Then on with strip Settlers of Catan.

A crash from the kitchen.

JOHNNY: Everything okay in there?

CHARM: (*yelling from the kitchen in a disguised voice*) Yup yup yup. Just using my manual labour skills to complete some manual labour.

FAITH: You must have a really solid condo board
to send someone in the middle of the night.

JOHNNY: I didn't even know we had a leak.

TEASEL: So Moxy's not coming home?

JOHNNY: Oh, she'll be home.
Reeking of disappointment
and looking to take it out on me.

TEASEL: Until then, we've got the time to get a little closer.

FAITH: Just say the word and we'll split.

A key in the door.

JOHNNY: What? No! Moxy!

FAITH: My shirt!

HEARTFREE: My pants!

JOHNNY: The closet.
Quick!

FAITH and TEASEL scramble into the closet.

MOXY stumbles in half-naked, covered in vomit and blood.

Moxy! You're home early.

MOXY: Could have gone longer,
could have gone harder
but a friend showed me a video
that made me think of you.

JOHNNY: Oh . . . that's nice.

MOXY: You're alone.

JOHNNY: Yes . . . of course. Well, Heartfree's here.

MOXY: But he doesn't really count.

HEARTFREE: Hey.

MOXY: Unless he gets his dick out of his hand
and makes a move.

HEARTFREE: Hey.

MOXY: What? I thought you were fluid.

HEARTFREE: Well . . . yeah . . . in theory.

MOXY: Uh, it's just too easy.

JOHNNY: You're bleeding.

MOXY: Just the tracks of a night well lived.

JOHNNY: I'll get the bandages.

MOXY: I'm fine.

JOHNNY: I hate to see you bleed.

MOXY: Then get me a razor and I'll open up my wrists.

JOHNNY: Honestly, Moxy—

MOXY: Honestly, Johnny, you use the word honest
in every other sentence.

JOHNNY: And you've started policing everything I say.

MOXY: Because it all sounds to me like a load of bull.

JOHNNY: Is it really so hard to take me at my word.

MOXY: It's these damn times we live in.
Too much irony to take anything for truth.

JOHNNY: You don't look good.

MOXY: See. Now how am I supposed to believe that.

JOHNNY: You look sick.

MOXY: I always look good.

JOHNNY: Let's get you off to bed.

MOXY: Trying to get rid of me, are you?

JOHNNY: We all should get some rest.

MOXY: All?

   Beat.

Kiss me.

JOHNNY: What?

MOXY: I can't go to bed without a goodnight kiss.

He reluctantly kisses her.

JOHNNY: There, now off to bed.

MOXY: I make you sick, is that it?

JOHNNY: No.

MOXY: I make you want to vomit.

JOHNNY: Of course not.

MOXY: Good.
Kiss me again.

JOHNNY: I . . . think . . . we'd better—

MOXY: Can't kiss your wife?

JOHNNY: It's not that.

MOXY: On our anniversary, no less.

JOHNNY: You're the one who—

MOXY: You like to leave me hanging?

JOHNNY: No.

MOXY: Just slouching here with no self-esteem.

JOHNNY: Of course not.

MOXY: Baby, I need my self-esteem.

JOHNNY: Moxy—

MOXY: Kiss me.

He does.

Now that wasn't much of a make-out.

JOHNNY: I'm tired, Moxy.

MOXY: Anyone would think you didn't love me anymore. What do you think, Heartfree?

HEARTFREE: Huh?

MOXY: Don't you think Johnny's being a little bit standoffish tonight?

HEARTFREE: It's late, Moxy.

MOXY: Oh, did he get his period?

HEARTFREE: Come on, Moxy, we were just getting ready for bed.

MOXY: Kiss me.

JOHNNY: Moxy—

*MOXY gives JOHNNY a full-body make-out.
She rubs vomit and blood all over him
and starts to take off his clothes.*

MOXY: Now that you're just as filthy as me,
let's muck each other out like a couple of pigs.
(*snort!*)

JOHNNY: Moxy, please.

MOXY: Come on, let's "make love."

JOHNNY: Moxy—

MOXY: Right here.

JOHNNY: But Heartfree.

MOXY: He can join in.

HEARTFREE: I should go.

JOHNNY: I'm not going to—

MOXY: Do it.

JOHNNY: I'm not going to—

MOXY: Do it.

JOHNNY: Moxy, NO!

    Beat.

MOXY: Okay.

JOHNNY: I'm sorry.

MOXY: All right.

JOHNNY: I didn't mean to—

MOXY: Stop.

Beat.

I am tired.

JOHNNY: I know.

MOXY: So tired.

JOHNNY: Go to bed.

MOXY: Okay.

JOHNNY: Good. Great. Good.

She goes for the closet.

Wait! Where are you going?

MOXY: I left my charger in the pocket of my coat.

JOHNNY: Use mine.
It's on the nightstand.

MOXY: But what will you use, my love?

JOHNNY: I think I have an extra.

MOXY: I'll just get mine.

JOHNNY: The closet door is broken.

MOXY: Really?

JOHNNY: Jammed. Yeah. I'll fix it tomorrow.

CHARM emerges from the kitchen.

CHARM: I could fix that for you now.

MOXY: Who are you?

JOHNNY: He's here for the pipes.

MOXY: What's wrong with the pipes?

JOHNNY: Don't worry about the closet.

CHARM: I'm sure it will only take a second.
Let me get my tool.
The proper tool for the proper job,
is what I always say.

CHARM walks out with an enormous sledgehammer.

JOHNNY: Honestly, I can deal with it tomorrow.

CHARM: I find brute force is most useful
in these situations.

He raises the sledgehammer above his head.

MOXY: Maybe I'll just try to open it first.

CHARM: If you wanna go the layman's route.

MOXY opens the door.
TEASEL and FAITH are squished inside.

TEASEL: Oh, hey Moxy.

MOXY: Ladies, ladies, ladies.
Hasn't history taught us that the closet is not the place
for making out.

TEASEL: Ha ha.

MOXY: Just get it out in the open,
you know what I mean?

TEASEL: Uproar.

MOXY: Kidding, kidding.
What do I owe you?

TEASEL: What do you mean?

MOXY: I mean, what's the going rate?

TEASEL: For what?

MOXY: For proving that my husband isn't as honest as he pretends
to be.

FAITH: Listen, Moxy—

MOXY: Seriously. Thanks, Faith.

FAITH: However strange this seems
I think we should all just exercise mindfulness
and remember that every action has a cause and effect.

MOXY: I'm sorry, are you talking butterflies?

FAITH: You treat him like shit.

MOXY: Great.

FAITH: You can barely look at him without rolling your eyes.
You can't say anything to him
without scorn on your breath.
You can't treat someone that way.

MOXY: And what do you know about marriage?
I, for one, can't remember the last man
I saw panting after you.
Have you ever had a boyfriend, Faith?

TEASEL: Easy, Moxy.

MOXY: Have you ever had a fuck to hold onto?

TEASEL: Moxy!

MOXY: Honestly, Teasel, help me out here.
She reads self-help books and celebrity blogs
and thinks she's an expert on relationships.
Thinks she's an expert on love.
Getting my husband to pop her cherry in the park.

JOHNNY: But nothing actually happened, Moxy.

FAITH: It's true. I mean, I tried, I'll admit it,
but your husband is an honest guy.

MOXY: Honest, yeah, so I keep hearing.

TEASEL: Nothing happened, Moxy.

JOHNNY: It's the truth.
I swear it.
Nothing actually happened.

TEASEL: They were helping me.

MOXY: What are you talking about?

TEASEL: I've been . . . courting . . . I guess is a word for it.
Falling pretty deeply, actually,
into being into Heartfree.

CHARM drops the sledgehammer on his toe.

CHARM: Not to worry. I'm a professional.

TEASEL: I knew if you knew, you'd be on us like a hawk,
picking the life out of whatever was being born
and I just wanted time, I guess.

MOXY: For what?

TEASEL: To see where this thing goes
before testing it with your scorn and sarcasm.

MOXY: You and Heartfree?

TEASEL: Johnny and Faith were just helping us hide the truth.

MOXY: He's a loser though, right, you know that?

TEASEL: But you got me, Moxy.
Nothing crawls past you unscathed
so take the piss.
Fair play.

MOXY looks at them.

MOXY: Let's see it then.

TEASEL: See what?

MOXY: This burgeoning love.
I want to see the look.

TEASEL: What look?

MOXY: The look of love.
Or lust.
Or whatever you kids call it these days.

HEARTFREE: You want us to look at one another?

MOXY: You can go at it too, if the mood takes you.

JOHNNY: They're not going to stand here and make out
just so you can—

MOXY: Why not?

JOHNNY: Because it's—

MOXY: Immoral?

JOHNNY: No, because it's—

MOXY: Crass?

JOHNNY: No, well, yes, but—

MOXY: Because they're spreading it thick to cover for you.

Beat.

TEASEL: All right.

HEARTFREE: All right?

TEASEL: I mean, if you don't mind . . .

HEARTFREE: No . . . I mean, yeah . . .
I'm cool.

> *They look at each other.*
> *They kiss.*

MOXY: Oh, come on!
Any piss-drunk kid in a bar could have done the same.

TEASEL: Well, we're not going to stand here making out
until you're satisfied.

MOXY: You're not?
Okay.
Then maybe Faith and Johnny want to give it a try.

JOHNNY: What do you mean?

MOXY: If your relationship is as platonic as you say,
your kiss will be as unpolished as that sorry display of nerves.

JOHNNY: But I haven't—

MOXY: Okay, but maybe you want to.
Maybe you should.
Maybe you need to see what it would feel like
to blow fluff from a dandelion.

JOHNNY: Stop.

MOXY: To cuddle a kitten as the sun goes down.

FAITH: Stop!

MOXY: To gaze and tilt and sigh and whisper,
so let's see you give it a try.

JOHNNY: Stop it, Moxy.

MOXY: I want to see you give it a try.

JOHNNY: Moxy!

MOXY: You're clearly attracted to her.

JOHNNY: Of course I'm attracted to her!

   Beat.

I mean, look at her.
She is unbelievably hot.
Look at those . . . sparkling eyes,
that . . . generous smile,
that incredibly gorgeous body.
Half the time when I'm talking to her,
I'm not listening to a word she's saying because
I'm thinking about what it would feel like
to rub my hands all over her—
sorry to objectify you, like this, Faith—

FAITH: No, yeah, sure, that's okay.

JOHNNY: You want me to kiss her?
You want to see me give it a try?
I'll do it.
I'll gladly do it, but if I do,
for me, that's the end of us.

I can't live like this, Moxy.
I've been trying and waiting and asking and listening
and hoping and giving and fighting for this marriage because,
for some insane reason,
I love you.

There is something about you
that feels essential to my essential self
and for me, that's important.
But if you think that's stupid,
or if you just don't feel the same way,
or if you can't make the time to hear me
and see me and let yourself need me
then I have to find someone who can.

It's up to you, Moxy.
Should I kiss Faith?
Do you really want to see me try?

    Long beat.

MOXY: We should . . .

    Long beat.

. . . talk about this.

JOHNNY: What?

MOXY: If you want.
We should . . . talk about this.

JOHNNY: Okay.

Beat.

CHARM: *(removing his disguise)* You make me sick.

ALL: Charm Lefou?!

CHARM: You know I sacrificed my integrity for you.
For all of you.
Dressed up like a lowly manual labourer
who does manual labour to try to stop you all
from making fools of yourselves, but look at you . . . fools.

And if you're thinking I'm green to the gills with jealousy,
wishing I were you, Heartfree,
getting into it with you, Teasel,
you are deeply mistaken.
You haven't got a clue.
I acted out of pity for you both.
To spare you the suffering that will no doubt ensue
when you start to date one another.
But I can tell by the looks on your faces
that none of you seem to have the capacity for gratitude.

In fact, the only person who is truly loyal to me,
truly devoted to understanding the sacrifice
of my offerings is Mimi.
A sweet, gentle, Québécoise girl
who has watched in disgust
as the lot of you have carried on with your vulgarities.
Lord knows what stories she'll bring back to La Belle Province.

> *CHARM opens the door to leave.*
> *MIMI and RAZ are making out in the hall.*

Mimi!
Mimi!

CHARM pushes past them.

Viens, Mimi!

MIMI: Non, merci!

She smiles and closes the door.

TEASEL: So . . . you want to get dinner sometime?

HEARTFREE: Sure, yeah, great.
And there's a band I've been wanting to check out
if you . . .

TEASEL: Oh . . . cool.

HEARTFREE: Yeah?

TEASEL: Okay.

Lights out on everyone but MOXY.

SCENE 5—TRUTH IS DIFFERENT THAN HONESTY

MOXY: *(to audience)* Truth is different than honesty.
Truth is howling yourself into the night,
and screaming your contradictions.
It's hurting people,
provoking others to hurt you,
getting hurt and feeling hurt,
and saying you've been hurt
and finding a way to get over that hurt
to do it all again.

It's spilling blood on the floor
and rubbing it into the windows,
so every time you look outside
you remember what it cost to find the truth.

I did feel something.
Just now.
A weight in my chest.
A squeezing in my stomach.
A flurry of desire and frustration and fear and pain
and I didn't know what to say.
I was paralyzed.
And it was . . . a release?

Didn't think he had it in him.

I wonder if marriage is some sort of radical proposal for our age.
Instead of a shackling or a deadening
or a sacrifice to the gods of capitalism,
could marriage possibly be an antidote
to instant gratification?

A slow and steady deepening?
An erosion of insecurity?
A return to sensation?
An admission of the endless confusion
that takes us from day to day.

EPILOGUE

EVERYONE IS HAPPY

Lights up on CHARM *at his synthesizer.*
As he sings this song, individual spotlights rise slowly, one by
one, on all the other characters.
Each is in his/her own space listening to the song.
Without irony, everyone joins the chorus looking out at the
audience.
Perhaps they even encourage the audience to join in or clap.
It should feel triumphant.

CHARM: Everyone is happy.
Everyone is fine.
Everyone is posting things
about having a fabulous time.

Nobody's lonely.
No one's upset.
No one's expecting things
to be constantly laced with regret.

Sometimes I'm tempted
to think the world is just unfair,
to leave me stranded with my dreams
and feeling unaware.
I stare into the mirror
and feel like a disgrace.
It's then that I remember
to take a photo of my face.

Because . . .

Everything is awesome.
Everything is cool.
Everything is happening,
and nobody looks like a fool.

Everyone is happy.
Everyone is fine.
Everyone is posting things
on each other's things all the time.

EVERYONE IS HAPPY!

SMOKE

ELENA BELYEA

To Kristina and Geoffrey

ACKNOWLEDGEMENTS

Thank you to Andrea, Christine, Jenna, Mom, and Dad.

PLAYWRIGHT'S NOTE

I began writing this play in March 2016, around the time Canadian media personality Jian Ghomeshi was being acquitted of all charges (four counts of sexual assault and one count of choking). I had just seen Will Eno's *The Realistic Joneses* at Theatre Network in Edmonton, and unprecedented wildfires had dominated the news the summer prior.

I wrote two scenes (now scenes two and three), which I submitted in my application to Nightwood Theatre's 2016–2017 Write From the Hip Playwriting Unit with director/dramaturg Andrea Donaldson at the helm. Two and a half years later, I had the immense joy of watching *Smoke* come to life courtesy of Calgary's Downstage in February 2019. (The amazing team, to whom I am eternally indebted, is listed on the next page.) Rehearsing and premiering *Smoke*'s inaugural production was a uniquely awesome and humbling experience.

But it was also painful. In my experience, writing a play is often lonely work, but *Smoke* was especially isolating. I was incredibly anxious any time the piece was about to be heard or seen by a new audience. After it premiered, there were many times when folks offered reactions to the piece that took me months, and in some cases years, to unpack. While some of these comments were disappointing, if not heartbreaking, others were hopeful and life-changing, and continue to affect me and my writing practice to this day.

In its first iterations, *Smoke* was a conversation between a cisgender (someone whose gender identity matches the sex they were assigned at birth) woman (Aiden) and a cisgender man (Jordan). However, I quickly realized I wanted to create something that aligned more closely with my lived experience as a queer, pansexual, non-binary femme/woman. I sought to make room for a cis woman/cis woman variation within the script as well. (My intention was not to assert that gender is a binary, as this is not my experience—I address this more explicitly in the Notes section.) So, I worked to create two versions of the play housed in one text, so Jordan could be played as a cis woman, a cis man, and/or both as part of the same production. This is how it was staged for its premiere: with the same actor playing Aiden each night and two separate actors alternating the role of Jordan between performances. I've also tried to write it so that Aiden and Jordan's relationship has queer undertones, no matter what the casting, inviting space for the possibility that Aiden and/or Jordan might be bi or pansexual in both iterations.

After watching the aforementioned versions run simultaneously, I believe the play exists clearly and energetically in both configurations, but that the piece comes from seeing or reading the two iterations with an awareness of the other. I believe audiences hear lines differently if they're considering what it would be like to hear them spoken by someone of another gender. At its core, I believe *Smoke* is a play about two people whose lives have changed irrevocably by separate traumatic events and who are both trying to figure out how to move on.

As a playwright, I try to write plays that ask questions instead of providing answers (I have none). Some of the questions *Smoke* poses: What's an apology and what makes it meaningful? How does a person's race, class, sexuality, gender, and ability affect their access to healing? What would it take for me to forgive someone I love after a betrayal? To what lengths would I go to support the healing of someone I loved, even if that meant I could no longer be a part of their life?

In my own life, the complexity, urgency, and messiness around conversations about sexual violence, consent, accountability, restorative justice, and rehabilitation have only amplified in recent years. *Smoke* has been a place for me to put my questions.

CRUCIAL CONVERSATIONS: SOCIAL LOCATION AND POWER IN *SMOKE*

JENNA RODGERS

Long before I was officially involved in the first production of *Smoke*, Elena and I had a burgeoning friendship and a mutual respect for each other's creative practices. We met at the Banff Centre when Elena was still a student at the National Theatre School and I was in my first year as associate dramaturg with the Playwrights Lab. I had been following Elena's work with great interest and was impressed with how they navigated gender issues in complex ways, but for this project they were proposing to explore the intersections of gender with race by featuring an Asian character.

I am a mixed-race Chinese Canadian artist, and when Elena (a white artist) asked for my feedback on their script, they made it clear to me that I was not being approached simply because of my ethnicity. One of my side hustles is as an equity, diversity, and inclusion facilitator (I'm now shifting my language toward an anti-racist practice, but at the time EDI was the vocabulary I was working with). I reckoned this would be an opportunity to dip my toe into the world of cultural consultation with an artist I trusted, while working as a dramaturg, a role that I love.

What was unexpected to me was how my practice as a facilitator helped me answer cultural questions provoked by the script, which were never so much questions about Asian-ness, but rather about how a racialized person might feel when power is stacked against them. Throughout *Smoke*, Jordan's power is stacked against Aiden's—Jordan is white, upper middle-class, and, in some productions, cis male (among other identifications).[1] We must hold these identifiers in opposition to Aiden, who is Asian, working class, and cis female. The play is never about a single instance of racism, but rather about how the power imbalance offers Jordan opportunities that Aiden is unable to access. Thinking about how we could parse this imbalance as a company led us to utilize language in the rehearsal hall that I often use in my work outside of it, in facilitation around ideas of social location.

Social location refers to the lines that have been constructed in the fabric of society to help group people into common categories such as (but not limited to) gender, race, class, age, disability, religion, sexual orientation, and language. These lines are *socially constructed*, meaning that they are the product of collective views that are developed and maintained within our society. A person's social location is the combination of categories they belong to because of their identity, placing individuals in relationship to each other, to power, and to the "dominant" culture. *Smoke* investigates the intersections of many cruxes of power: race, gender, sexual orientation, class, religion—much more than Aiden's Asian-ness is explored.

As a writer, Elena is well aware of their own social location and, through their writing, seeks to find ways to engage with identities outside of their lived experience—something writers have done for generations, but something that is increasingly complex as debates about art, ownership, and appropriation unfold within the fast-paced world of social media and call-out culture. Who has the right to tell a story? Unfortunately, there is no easy answer to this question. Writers must grapple with their responsibility as storytellers, find ways to engage meaningfully with communities they wish to write about, and be prepared to speak to their creative decisions when questions arise—because we must assume questions will arise.

---

1   The script indicates that Jordan can be played by a cisgender male or female actor. The first production cast both, alternating in the role through the run. As Elena Belyea notes in their preface to the play, trans, non-binary, and/or gender non-conforming actors could also be cast, and they are open to exploring these possibilities with creative teams wishing to produce the play in this way.

During the development process of *Smoke,* Elena mentioned that this play was part of their exploration of the complex conversations surrounding sexual assault within queer communities—particularly how they differ from heteronormative culture's understandings of sexual assault. They expressed that they didn't expect the script to resonate with everyone. I remember thinking that was a pity. It's a pity that we've been trained to believe that our work can only be seen or valued by people who experience similar injustice. This is not without reason. Power structures and systems are designed to maintain a status quo. It is the work of the artist to disrupt the status quo, to introduce new ideas into the zeitgeist, and to provoke conversation in the audience.

I am sitting down to write this introduction at a strange time. It is August 2020, and now, more than ever, we are in need of art that responds to the contemporary condition and asks big questions of society. We are living amid a great pause, a time at which a virus has radically shifted our daily rhythms. Some of us have had more time, some of us have had less, but amid it all, people are dying. And not just from COVID-19. This time has offered us the space and clarity required to process the generational slaughtering of Black and Indigenous peoples across Turtle Island. With Ahmaud Arbery, we thought, "going for a jog; that would never happen in Canada," and with Breonna Taylor, we thought, "police home invasions in the night—not here!" and with George Floyd, we thought, "yikes . . . maybe there is a problem." But then there were Regis Korchinski-Paquet, and Chantel Moore, and Rodney Levi . . . The list goes on.

People are dying, and we must resist the urge to lay singular blame and point singular fingers. We live in a system that perpetuates injustice, and we must spend time investigating our complicity. Elena's script does an excellent job of inviting the audience to question their biases. If you have the opportunity to see *Smoke,* witness it twice. Clock how you feel. Think about what we've been taught about gender. About race. About sex. About sexual violence. Clock how you feel again. And then consider making a donation to an organization that supports queer survivors of sexual assault so that the conversation initiated in the theatre has a meaningful impact outside of it.

WHERE THERE'S *SMOKE*...
THEA FITZ-JAMES

"Where there is smoke, there's fire" typically means that if there is a rumour about someone, there is potentially some truth to it. The smoke is both proof of the fire and something of a fire itself by proxy. You don't need to see the fire to believe it exists. You just need the smoke.

I am not trying to be pedantic with my exploration of the aphorism; instead, I argue that the assumptions of the smoke-fire proxy are deconstructed in Elena Belyea's one-act play *Smoke*. Two former partners, Aiden and Jordan, have an unceremonious meeting in Aiden's Calgary apartment, where Jordan confronts Aiden about an accusation of sexual assault. The play is framed and interrupted by Aiden reading a story about a small town that keeps catching fire, a story that she is writing during the action of the play and completes by the end of the play. Similarly, Jordan reads poetry at a book launch six months after their meeting, with his/her poetry punctuating the evening the two spend together. As such, their conversation plays out in queer time. Queer time, which challenges linear, normative temporalities rooted in heteropatriarchy and capitalism, is "at best contrapuntal, syncopated, and at worst, erratic, arrested" (McCallum and Tuhkanen 1). In performance, queer time can "move backward, lunge forward, loop, jump, stack, stop, pause, linger, elongate, pulsate, slip" (Pryor 9). This concept is at work in the different ways that Aidan and Jordan have measured the two years between their previous meeting and the moment we meet them in the play. But queer time can fracture form as well as content: arguments in the present resurrect a horrible night in the past, while poems read in the future complicate things to come, in real time. What is the relationship between the past and the current moment, and how does that influence the future staged for the audience now? Is this arrested development or foreshadowing? These questions linger around a story that to many may seem timeless: the story of sexual assault, rape, and violence against women.[1]

Smoke explores many of the contemporary concerns that have come to the forefront in the wake of the #MeToo Revolution. Issues of consent, sex, and believability are wound together and spark, offering more questions than answers as the characters navigate their first reunion after two years of silence. The demand for accountability, confidentiality, and a "real" apology meets the easy banter sometimes found with an ex-lover after so many years, serving as a reminder that some waters run deep, that buried fires still burn. These complications colour the characters' believability. What is deemed "true" in sexual assault cases—either public or private—often becomes the focus, with many laurels resting on the binary of she-said-he-said. This gendered turn of phrase cannot possibly capture the nuance of sexual violence. And yet, legislative bodies and, indeed, much of the justice system, rely on he-said-she-said testimony; entire arguments, cases, and trials hinge on burden of proof and reliability. Putting the embodied experience of rape into this legislative logic is akin to putting a round peg in a square hole, begging questions around whether judicial methodologies are effective (or appropriate) in dealing with questions of sexual violence. And yet, Canadian judicial systems so often ask survivors to contort themselves, carving their round edges into corners until they fit—albeit smaller than they were when they started. Taking a restorative justice approach to sexual assault ideally invites contradictory truths to coexist—it is not important to determine who is telling the "truth," but rather to ask how to heal the harm done—with the caveat

---

1   Editor's Note: In the play, as in this introduction, the terms "sexual assault" and "rape" are both employed. Each term comes with its own historical, cultural, and politicized usage, with the former being used as a legal term in Canada to encapsulate (and validate) a range of experiences of sexual violence. Both terms are used by some survivors to name their experiences as an important part of their process of identifying and healing.

that these initiatives are survivor-led.[2] This is where I position myself: as a survivor, as a queer woman, as an activist committed to engaging in how we can begin to create communities of accountability.[3] Going beyond simply the lip service of calling-in,[4] *Smoke* explores both how trauma lingers and love lasts and ultimately how these contradictions can coexist. Breaking the binary of he-said-she said (or she-said-she-said), the audience are invited not to judge, but to witness, and in so doing, to question their own gendered assumptions and biases.[5]

While believability is central to the play's action, I'd like to posit that *Smoke* is not interested in what the "truth" is. Just like Aiden's story, this isn't a play about the "truth" of what happened. "This is a story about what came after." Belyea invites us to think not about what started the town fires, but what the townsfolk do with the ash; she explores not the origin of sexual assault, but what to do with the relationship afterwards. "Where there is smoke, there's fire"—surely we can all assume that this is "true"? And yet, Belyea's *Smoke* queers this linear equation. Instead, where there is smoke, there is sex. There is love. There is discourse. There is some kind of a meeting, between two things in friction, between two bodies, between two people in love. By escaping the reductive linear logic (and time) of smoke equals fire, *Smoke* invites different possibilities between Aiden and Jordan. And in these possibilities, we might find healing, redemption, and forgiveness. Aiden's story of fire is juxtaposed against Jordan's endless Vancouver rain. But as the play reminds us, when a town catches fire, it's not always as simple as putting it out. And more importantly, it's not only rain that falls from the sky.

2   The foundational text on restorative justice is *The Revolution Starts at Home: Confronting Intimate Violence within Activist Communities*, edited by Ching-In Chen, Jai Dulani, and Leah Lakshmi Piepzna-Samarasinha.

3   For more on this work, see Fitz-James's "Consent on the Fringe: Restorative Justice and Accountable Communities."

4   "Calling in"—in opposition to calling out—is the practice of pointing to the harm someone has done in such a way as to invite them "in" to a process of healing, accountability, and ultimately mutual understanding.

5   Given that the characters in the play are specifically gendered male or female, and that the play itself is discussing the gendered assumption around sexual assault with the invitation to cross cast, I believe the gendered phrase "he-said-she-said" or "she-said-she-said" is particularly appropriate in discussing this play.

WORKS CITED

Chen, Ching-In, Jai Dulani, and Leah Lakshmi Piepzna-Samarasinha, editors. *The Revolution Starts at Home: Confronting Intimate Violence within Activist Communities*. South End, 2011.

Fitz-James, Thea. "Consent on the Fringe: Restorative Justice and Accountable Communities." *Canadian Theatre Review*, vol. 180, 2019, pp. 14–19. http://dx.doi.org/10.3138/ctr.180.003.

McCallum, E.L., and Mikko Tuhkanen, editors. Introduction. *Queer Times, Queer Becomings*. SUNY, 2011, pp. 1–21.

Pryor, Jaclyn. *Time Slips: Queer Temporalities, Contemporary Performance, and the Hole of History*. Northwestern UP, 2017.

Smoke was developed through Nightwood Theatre's 2016–2017 Write From the Hip Playwriting Unit with support from Program Director and Dramaturg Andrea Donaldson, as well as the unit's other participants: Michelle Langille, Lisa Ryder, Deanna Kruger, Gitanjali Lena, and Hannah Rittner.

It received a staged reading as part of Nightwood's Groundswell Festival in Tkarón:to (Treaty 13 territory, Toronto) on September 27, 2017, where it was read by Diana Luong (Aiden) and Jesse LaVercombe (Jordan).

Smoke premiered at Downstage in Moh'kins'tsis (Treaty 7 territory, Calgary) with one cast on February 13, 2019, (Chantelle Han and Joel David Taylor) and again on February 14, 2019, (Chantelle Han and Alexandra Dawkins).

The cast and production team comprised of:

Aiden: Chantelle Han
Jordan (F): Alexandra Dawkins
Jordan (M): Joel David Taylor

Director: Christine Brubaker
Stage Manager: Carissa Sams
Dramaturg: Andrea Donaldson
Production Dramaturg: Jenna Rodgers
Lighting Designer: Graham Frampton
Sound Designer: Thomas Geddes
Set Designer: Anton DeGroot
Costume Designer: Jordan Wieben
Production Manager: Jessie Paynter
Production Assistant: Katherine Penhale
University of Calgary Theatre Intern: Ivanna Ihekwoaba

SETTING

Aiden's apartment. Calgary (Moh'kins'tsis, Treaty 7).
A bookstore during Jordan's book launch in Vancouver (the unceded lands of the xʷməθkʷəy̓əm (Musqueam), Sḵwx̱wú7mesh (Squamish), and səlil̓wətaʔɬ (Tsleil-Waututh) First Nations).

TIME

The scenes in Aiden's apartment take place in February 2019.

Jordan's book launch takes place nine months afterwards (November 2019). Aiden hears and/or reads Jordan's poems "Anxiety," "Nostalgia," and "Eulogy" in scene three. "Awakening" is the poem that Jordan writes to replace "Eulogy."

Aiden's completed fire story is being read after the main action of the play. These sections are written as direct address to the audience. There's no need to try and fit them into the naturalistic container of a public reading.

CHARACTERS

Aiden Lee: Twenty-three years old. Cisgender woman. Asian Canadian. Fiction writer. Working class. Lives alone. Parents are divorced. Closer with her father. Mother moved out when Aiden was seventeen. Three younger brothers. Well-read. Charismatic. Funny. Passionate. Articulate. Stubborn. Has high expectations of herself and those around her. Works part-time as a caterer.

Jordan Engels: Twenty-three years old. Can be played as a cisgender man or woman. (The script will indicate which lines are for which casting with either an M or F). Caucasian (half-Jewish). Poet. From a modestly wealthy family. One sister (Charlotte, nicknamed "Charlie"). Strained relationship with parents. Struggles with anxiety. Well-read. Self-deprecating. Self-identifies as an activist (can be gently implied through costume). Works for a realty firm, maintaining their website.

NOTES

Beats indicate a gearshift and possibly (though not necessarily) a brief pause. A pause is a short break, usually when the characters are recalibrating or on the precipice of a decision. A slash / indicates where in the current line the next character to speak should come in with their line.

In the premiere production, Aiden was played by a cisgender female-identified actor each night, while Jordan was played by a cisgender male-identified actor on night A and a cisgender female-identified actor on night B. My intention in crafting the script to accommodate both casting possibilities was to create an invitation for myself and others to investigate my and their personal biases when it comes to gender, consent, and sexual violence.

With that said, my intention is not to imply that gender or sex exist exclusively within the binary of "man" and "woman." (They are simply two of many possibilities). Based on my own lived experiences, these were the specific positions I wanted to explore in this play at the time of writing. I am open to exploring how the script could function with Aiden and/or Jordan as trans, non-binary, and/or otherwise gender non-conforming. However, this current draft does not account for the further complexity this would add to their conversation. If this is something you and your theatre company are interested in investigating, please reach out.

The desired effect is that the audience is invited to understand both characters' perspectives as much as possible. Both Aiden and Jordan must be certain their version of events is the truth. However, there is also room for moments of self-doubt. I believe it is important that there are instances when both Jordan and Aiden consider, if only privately and briefly, that the other might be right.

It's essential both characters are empathetic, reasonable, funny, and emotionally intelligent. A past version of the script said, "If either character is made to seem much less empathetic, reasonable, and/or likable than the other, the potency of the piece is compromised." While I still believe this to be true, I have also witnessed the extent to which an audience—particularly a white, older, middle/upper-class audience—will work to take Jordan's side. One thing that I have found to be effective is to make sure that Jordan, despite her/his moments of backtracking and many apologies, continues actively fighting to assert his/her version of the truth throughout the entire play. When in doubt, while establishing the "believability" of each character, I recommend leaning more heavily on Aiden's side of the scale to compensate for many viewers' unconscious predisposition to doubting survivors.

Lastly, the play's heavier moments must be countered with moments of laughter and lightness. Despite everything, Aiden and Jordan continue to greatly enjoy each other's company (though they may feel conflicted about this).

0.

Pre-show.

As the audience enters, AIDEN *sits at her computer in her base-ment studio apartment, trying to write.*

Mismatched furniture: a couch, desk, and chair. Shelves and shelves of books. Postcards, photos, and magazine cut-outs on the walls. Many plants, mostly succulents and cacti.

She procrastinates. She listens to music. She sits at her com-puter, then gets up and pours herself a glass of water. She drinks it. She sits back down and stares at her computer screen. She goes to the kitchen where she slices and eats an apple. She peers out her window. She checks her email. She looks some-thing up on her phone.

She stares at her computer screen.

1.

AIDEN stands and addresses the audience.

AIDEN: Once upon a time, there was a town: unremarkable and not without its problems, but the people who lived there were happy to call it home. The town's citizens spent their days buying groceries, walking their dogs, paying their phone bills, and fucking their part-ners, and generally speaking, life wasn't perfect, but it was good.

One day, a giant fire burned the entire town to the ground.

Historians will argue about its origins. If this was a different story, I would tell you possible theories include: an unattended stovetop, an electrical fire, lightning, amateur fireworks, arson. However, this isn't a story about what started the fire. This is a story about what came after.

As plumes of smoke blossomed overhead, sirens sounded, firefighters were dispatched, and planes released water over the all-you-can-eat buffet, pet store, and mid-range nail salon. Families piled into minivans, seeking refuge in nearby cities as a black haze descended, replacing the sun with a foreboding, far-off orange orb.

The rest of the country took pity, sending money transfers, cans of tomato soup, pyjama bottoms, two-for-one movie coupons, moist towelettes, shower caps, selfie sticks, and jars of pickled beets. Journalists came from all over, snapping hundreds of photos of the mayor with her shovel deep in the earth.

Bit by bit, the town was restored. People moved back into their houses, refilled their fridges, took their dogs for a quick pass around the lake, updated their smartphones, and learned new ways to have sex standing up.

Until one day, there was another fire, and again the town burned to the ground. Even though the citizens had just installed aluminum panels and cut down nearby trees to stop flames from jumping to their roofs, just in case. Reporters came, but not as many. And the rest of the country felt bad but had other causes that needed supporting.

Again, the town started over. And people tried to keep their spirits up, but some days, it was hard. Despite everything, the town's citizens hammered their hammers, and sawed their saws, and when they finished, objectively speaking, the town wasn't as impressive as it had been, but to the people who had rebuilt it, it was spectacular.

Then there was another fire.

2.

In the hallway outside AIDEN's *apartment,* JORDAN *knocks on* AIDEN's *door.* AIDEN *checks the peephole.*

AIDEN: *(under her breath)* Fuck!

JORDAN knocks again, louder this time. AIDEN paces.

(silently) Fuck, fuck, fuck, fuck, fuck, fuck, fuck!

JORDAN knocks again, ten times at least.

JORDAN: Hello? I'm looking for Aiden Lee.

Silence. Neither moves. Both listen. Eventually, JORDAN *takes out a notebook, tears out a page, writes a short message, and shoves it under the door.* AIDEN *stares at the note on the other side.*

JORDAN goes to leave down the apartment hallway. AIDEN *picks up and reads the note. When* JORDAN *has almost reached the stairwell:*

AIDEN: *(through the closed door)* How'd you get my address?

JORDAN: Sorry?

AIDEN: I asked, how the hell did you get my address?

JORDAN: Your dad.

AIDEN: Fuck, Jordan.

JORDAN: / I'm sorry, I—

AIDEN: What did you tell him?

JORDAN: That I needed to talk to you.

AIDEN: *(skeptical)* And he just gave you my address.

JORDAN: About something important.

AIDEN: *(sarcastic)* That's great. Thank you. Because he doesn't have enough on his mind.

JORDAN: I'm sorry. I didn't know how else to—

AIDEN: How'd you get inside the building?

JORDAN: The front door was open.

AIDEN: You're still supposed to buzz up.

JORDAN: I'm sorry, I didn't think / it would be—

AIDEN: That's the function of a buzzer, Jordan, it gives residents the opportunity to decide who they do and do not want to let inside the building.

JORDAN: On a related note: any chance of you letting me inside? Or would you prefer to continue this conversation through your closed door?

AIDEN: We are not having a conversation.

JORDAN: It won't take long.

AIDEN: I'm busy.

JORDAN: I can come back later.

AIDEN: I work later.

JORDAN: What about tomorrow?

AIDEN: I'm busy then too.

JORDAN: The day after that?

AIDEN: It's a jam-packed week for me.

JORDAN: I wouldn't have come all the way to Calgary if it wasn't important.

AIDEN: Generally speaking, if you send someone an email asking if they want to meet up, and they don't respond, it means they don't want to see you.

JORDAN: I thought maybe your spam filter—or that maybe you'd blocked my address / or something.

AIDEN: You should go.

JORDAN: Five minutes, Aiden, that's all I'm asking, please—

AIDEN: I just told you, I / don't want to—

JORDAN: I talked to Charmagne.

   Pause.

And she told me what you—not all of it. But some of it. And I thought about calling you, but figured, given the subject matter, it'd probably be better if we could talk in person. You know, face to face.

AIDEN: I don't want to talk to you.

JORDAN: You'd rather talk to our friends about me behind my back.

AIDEN: Yes. Exactly. Thank you.

JORDAN: Come on, Aiden. We should talk about it.

Beat.

I want to talk about it. Please.

Pause.

Final ask. If you really want me to go, I'll go. I just think it would be better if we could . . .

Silence. AIDEN exhales and then opens the door. Beat.

AIDEN: You coming in or what?

3.

JORDAN's book launch. JORDAN is simultaneously charismatic and deeply uncomfortable with public speaking.

JORDAN: Hi everyone. Thank you for coming. A big thank you to Green Moss and to (*referencing people in the audience*) Jill for the venue, Philip for putting this event together, and Amiri for the cover design. I'm going to read a few poems for you and if anyone wants to come by that table afterwards to buy a book, or chat, or whatever, I'll be there.

This first one is called, "Anxiety."

Beat.

My mother swears it's genetic.
Maybe there's some truth to this.
Epigeneticists claim trauma leaves
chemical markings on genes then passed on
to future generations.

My grandmother is roused by unfamiliar
voices cutting the warm night air.
Decades later, I wake with the feeling
of being hunted, spend the day
watchful as prey.

Our family resolves never to forget,
so children become connoisseurs of grief.
Bedside stories feature twins
in camps, bribed with sweets, amputated,
injected with illness.

My childhood is a rotted melon, basically,
a tooth swallowed by accident,
a split lip. An icy fall.
I keep a journal—that's one word for it—
a litany of youthful causes for concern.

At camp, I reject swimming lessons—
leeches have been known to enter any orifice.
School projects showcase bird flu,
malnourished polar bears, Vancouver's eventual collapse,
ocean lapping coolly at her demise.

Hypnotherapy is one solution.
Ativan is another, Prozac, Paxil, Zoloft.
I rehearse regulating my features
for the doctor in her swivel chair
prompting my trepidation with her stains.

A decade later, I wake with the feeling
of being hunted, and lie awake, still as prey,
escaped from unseen threats still lingering.
Invading headlights slash the peeling walls.
Until from the depths of sleep you sigh
a holy unintended saving breath.

4.

> AIDEN's *apartment.* AIDEN *stands as far from* JORDAN *as possible.* JORDAN *struggles to pull the door shut.*

JORDAN: Sorry, I can't . . . The door won't—

AIDEN: Throw your weight into it.

> JORDAN *tries and fails.*

God, let me.

> AIDEN *comes and bodychecks the door shut.*

JORDAN: I like your / place.

AIDEN: Let's just get this over with.

JORDAN: Okay.

> *Beat.*

Do you want to start or should I?

AIDEN: What exactly did Charmagne tell you?

JORDAN: That you called her out of the blue to catch up a couple weeks ago when you were in Victoria. And that during your conversation, you told her that something not . . . okay happened between us—sexually—back when we were together. And I didn't know what she was . . .

AIDEN: Did she happen to mention why she felt it was appropriate to share this information, which I had told her in confidence?

JORDAN: She said she wanted to give me a chance to "explain my actions." And when I tried to find out more, she said I should ask you myself. So, here I am.

(lightly) Let's just say it was not the conversation I was expecting when she texted saying she was in Vancouver and did I want to hit up our favourite falafel place.

    Beat.

What specifically were you referring to?

    Pause.

AIDEN: You're telling me you don't . . .

JORDAN: What?

AIDEN: You don't remember . . .

JORDAN: Remember what?

AIDEN: Yeah, this isn't—

Beat.

I don't want to do this.

JORDAN: Aiden, if I did something when we were together that wasn't okay, I want to know.

AIDEN: Why?

JORDAN: So I can apologize.

Pause.

AIDEN: You're telling me you don't remember anything?

JORDAN: Any of what?

AIDEN: You're telling me you don't remember sexually assaulting me at our graduation party.

JORDAN: I'm sorry, what?!

AIDEN: At Elise's house, end of fourth year.

JORDAN: Sorry, I remember the party, but I don't—

AIDEN: In Elise's bed.

JORDAN: I mean—we had sex, but that was consensual, we were both—

AIDEN: I was unconscious.

JORDAN: / What!?

AIDEN: And when I woke up you were—inside me. And when I told you to stop, and you wouldn't—

JORDAN: / I am so sorry, but I don't—

AIDEN: Until I asked multiple times.

JORDAN: Aiden, I'm sorry, but that is not how I—I mean—we were talking, / and checking in, with each other the whole—

AIDEN: I was passed out, how / would I have been able to—

JORDAN: And you were the one who initiated—

AIDEN: No, I didn't!

JORDAN: Fuck, fuck, okay, I just—remember? I was in the living room when you came up and asked if we could go somewhere more private? Maggie was DJing and wanted us to stay until that remix of "Ashes to Ashes" / had finished because Bowie had just died—

AIDEN: What the fuck does this have to do with anything?

JORDAN: Then you brought me upstairs and wanted to hook up, but we had just had that big fight about Berlin, and I wanted to talk about it. So, we talked about it, not a lot, but enough that it felt like everything was . . . okay. So, afterwards, when we started fooling around, and you offered to . . . go down on me, I was into it. And I was sitting in that office chair, which kept rolling around, which we both thought was really funny—

AIDEN: And after that—

JORDAN: We climbed into Elise's bed and you pulled me on top of—

AIDEN: No, no, no—that is not what happened!

JORDAN: I mean . . . Okay.

Beat.

What do you remember?

AIDEN: I remember getting to Elise's, and it being really uncomfortable, because everyone kept coming up and congratulating you about Germany. But I didn't want to let this fight ruin my graduation party, so I tried to have a good time. But I was still upset, so eventually I pulled you aside to ask if we could talk. And we talked. And I felt, like, not totally better, but better. And then we made out. And I, like—went down on you, and that was—fine. But then said I wasn't feeling feel well. And needed to lie down for a bit. So, I lay down and you lay down next to me. And when I woke up, you were . . . and wouldn't stop. Even after I . . .

JORDAN: Fuck. Fuck. I am so sorry, Aiden. Fuck. I just. There's no way I—

Beat.

The way I remember it, we lay down together, and you wanted to—

AIDEN: Should I bother going on, or would you like to keep telling me what I remember?

JORDAN: Sorry. I'm sorry.

Beat.

Then what?

AIDEN: Afterwards, we just lay there for a long time. And it was really awkward. Until eventually, I asked you what had just happened. And you got really upset. And started crying. A lot. And started to apologize.

JORDAN: I . . .

Beat.

Sorry, go on.

AIDEN: But then said you had to go to the bathroom, because you were gonna be sick. And you were gone for a while, and when you came back, you were a mess, like, weeping and drunker than I'd ever seen you. And when I tried talking to you, you couldn't understand anything I was saying. You asked if I wanted to take a cab home with you. I didn't. So, I spent the night at Elise's and walked home the next morning. Then, you texted, asking if I wanted to get breakfast. And I felt—like, on one hand, I really wanted to believe that I'd somehow misinterpreted—because you're right—this was the kind of thing I would have never thought that you . . . But I kept coming up against these three things: One—you had definitely had sex with me without asking, which—two—you definitely knew I was not okay with, and—three—I'd told you to stop. Clearly. Multiple times. And you didn't. So, I was like, okay, you want to talk? Let's talk. And we met up at Galaxy for breakfast. But when I asked, "Do you remember / what happened last night?"

JORDAN: "What happened last night?"

AIDEN: So, you remember.

JORDAN: I remember the conversation. But I thought you were talking about our fight.

AIDEN: No. I don't buy that.

JORDAN: So, I said sorry again about Berlin—

AIDEN: I remember the look on your face. You knew exactly what I was talking about.

JORDAN: No, Aiden—I swear, that's not—

AIDEN: Then I said, "Anything else?" And you / lied to my face.

JORDAN: Had no idea what you were talking about!

    Pause.

And then what? You just—

AIDEN: I went home.

JORDAN: And after that?

AIDEN: I left.

JORDAN: Like . . .

AIDEN: I packed up my stuff and flew back to Calgary.

JORDAN: Without telling anyone. What happened to driving back with your dad?

AIDEN: He wasn't coming until the weekend and I couldn't wait that long.

    Beat.

JORDAN: Fuck, Aiden. I am so sorry.

Beat.

Look, I know you probably won't—or, I don't know—don't believe me, but . . .

AIDEN: What?

JORDAN: And I'm not saying that you're not—I just—

(exhaling) I remember that night very clearly. Like, I've run it over in my head, like, a thousand times.

AIDEN: / So have I.

JORDAN: And I know that I didn't—

AIDEN: Then why did you send me that email the next day, trying to make up?

JORDAN: Because I could feel—things were still weird and—is this why you cut contact with me?

AIDEN: Obviously. Why else would I—

JORDAN: I had no idea! It was like—we go to this party, where everything seems—you know, like we have this fight but we made up, and as I remember it, still wound up having a good time.

AIDEN: *(sarcastic)* / Yeah, okay.

JORDAN: Then the next morning, it's like—we get breakfast, and plan to hang out after we're both finished packing. And the conversation's weird, but I figure it's because of grad, or our fight, or moving, or whatever. But the day after that, you won't respond to any of my texts or calls or emails, and when I go to your place, it's empty. Your landlord doesn't know anything. Your neighbours don't know anything. None of our friends or teachers know anything. You have vanished. I call your dad, he calls your mom, I file a missing person's report with the police. I go, like, twenty-four hours thinking that you're—that something very bad has happened to you. Until Taylor tells me you texted them, saying you're back in Calgary. And a couple hours after that, I see you've deleted me off of all your social media. And a couple hours after that, I get this cryptic email from you saying we're done. And no matter how many times I ask why, or try to get some kind of . . .

Beat.

So, yeah, I could tell I'd done something. But when you wouldn't give me any explanation—I thought maybe—I don't know—you were still mad about Berlin, you didn't want to do long-distance, you didn't want to be in a relationship now that we were done school, you didn't want to live with me, you didn't want to get married. All I knew for sure is that you didn't want anything to do with me, so eventually I had no choice but to leave you alone. I mean, for all intents and purposes, you ghosted me after a three-and-a-half-year relationship.

AIDEN: In my defence, I think I had a pretty good reason.

JORDAN: I just can't . . . like, the behaviour you're describing—I would I never, / not in a million years—

AIDEN: Even though it turns you on to engage sexually with unconscious partners?

JORDAN: Oh my God, Aiden, how many times do / we have to do this? That was completely different.

AIDEN: Do you or do you not like having sex with unconscious partners?

JORDAN: Sleep sex is not the same as having sex / with unconscious—

AIDEN: Answer the question.

JORDAN: Yes, being woken up with sex is a thing I enjoy.

AIDEN: And waking other people up—

JORDAN: Yes.

AIDEN: See?

JORDAN: You can have consensual sleep sex.

AIDEN: I never said you couldn't.

JORDAN: You have said that, explicitly, multiple times.

AIDEN: At the very least, it shows you're turned on by—

JORDAN: Aiden. It happened one time. When I was eighteen. My very limited sexual education failed me. It was really stupid of me, and I acknowledge I fucked up, and that I'm sorry. I have apologized for that one incident literally hundreds of times. But by the time I was twenty-one, at our graduation party, in the third year of our relationship, I definitely knew that behaviour was not okay, especially with you. So, if you're saying the one time I tried to initiate sleep sex with you in the second month of our relationship is conclusive evidence I sexually assaulted you at our graduation party two years ago, I'm sorry, but I disagree.

AIDEN: I just think it's important to acknowledge you have kind of a history.

JORDAN: I mean . . .

JORDAN exhales.

AIDEN: What?

JORDAN: Nothing.

Pause.

I mean . . . you don't feel like . . .

Beat.

AIDEN: What, Jordan?

JORDAN: On more than one occasion, your response to being upset about something was to get really drunk and try to have sex, then not remember it the next day.

AIDEN: / Oh my fucking God.

JORDAN: Which used to scare the shit out of me.

AIDEN: / Are you actually trying to tell me this is—

JORDAN: And you were really upset that night—

AIDEN: Yeah, because you accepted a residency we had applied for *together*, with the intention of doing *together*, without even—

JORDAN: No, I know—I just—I got the email and my knee-jerk reaction was to reply right away, which I know is no excuse, I was just excited—

AIDEN: And the thought of checking in with me before committing to two months in another country never crossed your mind?

JORDAN: I assumed you'd gotten in too!

AIDEN: Yeah, right—

JORDAN: You were the department superstar, Aiden, you got As on literally everything, even from McGee and she never gives As, meanwhile I was killing myself trying to maintain my B average—

AIDEN: Yeah, because I worked my ass off while you were getting high and reading *The Communist Manifesto*.

JORDAN: / That's not true and you know it.

AIDEN: I spent like, forty hours helping you edit that application.

JORDAN: I know. I'm sorry. I'm not trying to defend myself. I should have told you right away. But when I finally did, you were like, "It's fine, you should go," so I figured it was fine, until you spent the rest of the week making these passive aggressive comments—

AIDEN: No, I didn't—

JORDAN: "Have fun in Germany, I'll just be working the Stampede and getting heatstroke at the Lemon Heaven Stand!"

AIDEN: I was upset.

JORDAN: Then why didn't you just come out and say that?

AIDEN: I was trying to be supportive!

JORDAN: By lying to me?

AIDEN: I wasn't lying, I was genuinely trying to—why are we even talking about this?

JORDAN: What I'm trying to say is whenever we got into a fight and didn't have the time or space to actually address it, your way of trying to fix things was often by getting drunk and trying to connect physically.

AIDEN: You're making something that happened twice / out to be way more of a thing than it was.

JORDAN: More than twice.

AIDEN: / Fine, like—

JORDAN: That warehouse party in first year, Rae's birthday in second year, that club in Gastown—

AIDEN: / Okay, Jordan.

JORDAN: That New Year's party in fourth year, / Wordfest—

AIDEN: I get it.

JORDAN: You don't think there's any chance that maybe parts of what you remember aren't entirely—especially because everyone had a lot to drink that night—

AIDEN: Including you.

JORDAN: Including me. But you were—

AIDEN: If this was such a pattern of mine, why did you agree to have sex with me in the first place? By your account, I wasn't in any state to give actual consent.

JORDAN: But I was? You came onto me.

AIDEN: No, I didn't.

JORDAN: Are you sure you maybe didn't . . . Like, are you sure you remember . . .

Beat.

AIDEN: You think I blacked out.

JORDAN: I'm just trying to—

AIDEN: I didn't black out, Jordan. You, on the other hand—

JORDAN: No, I definitely remember—

AIDEN: So do I!

JORDAN: I just—

AIDEN: You call yourself a feminist! You are literally doing all the things you're not supposed to do. Victim blaming—

JORDAN: I'm just trying to—

AIDEN: Gaslighting—

JORDAN: I'm not—

AIDEN: Bringing up ancient history to make me doubt my experience: that's the definition of gaslighting!

JORDAN: Aiden, I'm sorry, this is just brand new information for me, I'm just trying to piece together exactly what happened—

AIDEN: I know what happened. I'm telling you what happened.

JORDAN: / I just—

AIDEN: I remember the blinds, I remember the stains on the ceiling, I remember the blue bed sheets, I remember the book on the bedside table, I remember I wasn't wearing my watch because the strap had just broken, I remember the shadows of the cars outside, I remember the light coming in under the door, I remember your hands, and your smell, and waking up with my underwear . . .

Pause.

JORDAN: Aiden, I'm so sorry.

AIDEN: If you were actually sorry, you would apologize.

JORDAN: But I didn't. I swear to God, I—

AIDEN: How do you know?

JORDAN: (*spiralling*) Is there any way we could get some kind of—like a—someone else, like, a mediator or something, like a neutral third party or—someone who has actual experience / dealing with this kind of—

AIDEN: What the fuck are you talking about?

JORDAN: I just feel like this situation is really fucked up, and confusing, and complicated, and like having someone else here to provide some kind of—I don't know—container / or framework for—

AIDEN: I don't want a mediator, Jordan, I want an apology.

JORDAN: I'm sorry for not checking in more before and during and afterwards, and for not realizing in the moment / that something wasn't—

AIDEN: No, like, an actual—

JORDAN: Obviously there was one, or several, moments of confusion between us that night; obviously, I played a part in that, and I'm sorry for any hurt I caused you. But it sounds like that's not what you're accusing me of. It sounds like you believe that I deliberately . . . raped you. And I did not do that. I would never do that to you or anyone else.

AIDEN: Why would I make this up?

JORDAN: I don't think you're making it up, I just—

AIDEN: You can't even admit there's a *possibility* that you—

JORDAN: No.

AIDEN: A possibility.

JORDAN: No.

AIDEN: How do you know?

JORDAN: I just do.

AIDEN: I'm not saying it was pre-meditated or that you're some kind of serial—

JORDAN: / I know that, but I—

AIDEN: But you made a choice, which had consequences.

JORDAN: / There's no way.

AIDEN: And if you actually want to make it better, you need to take responsibility—

JORDAN: Aiden, I'm sorry, but I can't. I mean, if we could go back or if we had some kind of—

AIDEN: Proof?

JORDAN: / That's not what I—

AIDEN: What proof am I supposed to have, Jordan? Should I have gone to the police, even though we were dating? Even though I'd just offered to perform oral sex on you? Should I have gone to the hospital and waited ten hours to do a rape kit, which [F: would have been testing for semen / M: would have very likely never been processed]? Or should I have assumed something like this would happen eventually and recorded all our sexual encounters, just in case?

JORDAN: I'm sorry, what I meant to say was—this is obviously a complex—

AIDEN: It's not, it's actually very straightforward.

JORDAN: There are just a number of different factors we need to— like, are you sure it wasn't someone else?

AIDEN: (*exploding*) Fuck, Jordan—

JORDAN: / Sorry, I'm sorry, I just—

AIDEN: You think I don't know the difference between your body and someone else's?

JORDAN: No, of course, I'm sorry, I'm just trying to, fuck—I don't know—make sure we investigate all the different possibilities here—

AIDEN: What happened to "believing survivors"?

JORDAN: I do—

AIDEN: / Evidently not.

JORDAN: I just also think the truth matters.

Beat.

Sorry, that definitely didn't come out right.

Pause.

AIDEN: *(with momentum)* You are such a fucking hypocrite, Jordan. You pretend to be this feminist, activist, ally; getting up on your social media high horse anytime someone gets called out for sexual assault—all those sprawling, self-righteous posts you made when Graham and the rest of the faculty was under investigation— preaching about survivor-led processes and rehabilitation and restorative justice. But suddenly when you're the one being called in, all of that goes out the window.

JORDAN: I'm sorry. That was a really fucked up thing to say. I am doing my best to practise what I preach here. But this is just a little overwhelming.

AIDEN: You're overwhelmed? You have no idea what the past two years have been like for me. I had to go back on antidepressants, I lost multiple jobs, I had to move in with my dad. And here you are, telling me the single most significant event of the past two years of my life didn't happen.

JORDAN: / Not that it didn't happen, just that—

AIDEN: You learn all the right vocabulary and read all the right books, so you can defend yourself with the right catchphrases and theorists and articles, making it impossible to believe someone like you could be capable of something like this. Because you're just not that kind of person. How about this? Any time I tell anyone about this from now on, I'll make sure whoever I'm talking to knows my "alleged" abuser has a completely different rendition of my "possible" rape and if they want to know about it, they can contact you, which I will hopefully have no idea how to do, after having the sublime pleasure of not seeing or speaking to you for years. Would that make you feel better?

Pause.

JORDAN: I mean . . . okay, Aiden.

Beat.

I'm really sorry. I wish that I could . . . But it doesn't sound like . . .

JORDAN heads for the door. Beat.

I'm gonna go. I'm sorry for bothering you.

AIDEN: You're running away.

JORDAN: I don't know what I'm supposed to do here, Aiden.

AIDEN: Do something. This is the situation. This is our situation.

JORDAN: I'm trying! But I can't accept responsibility for something I know I did not do. I wish I could. But I don't want to lie to you. I'm sorry. I'm sorry. I—do you want money? Can I pay for something—your meds, or your therapy, or the time you missed work—

AIDEN: You can't just throw your parents' money at all your problems, Jordan.

JORDAN: Not their money, my money, and I'm not—I'm just trying to—do something, like, anything, like an actual thing that is good. I mean, what do you want me to do? How can I make this better? I've tried apologizing, but I can't in the way that you—so, is there something else? Like, anything else that I can . . .

Beat.

Please.

Silence.

AIDEN: Three things. First, you're going to make a post on all your social media accounts, publicly acknowledging that you've been accused of sexual assault. Then you're going to make a donation to a centre that supports survivors of sexual violence. Then you're going to join a recovery group, so you can make sure this never happens again.

Handing JORDAN a pamphlet.

I checked online, Vancouver has the New Horizons Accountability and Support Network—

JORDAN: *(reading)* "The New Horizons Accountability and Support Network offers support for high-risk sex offenders who have served time in prison." Yeah, I don't think—

(reading) Also, it's through the Church. I'm sorry, Aiden, but I—

Beat.

I'll gladly make a donation somewhere. But I can't make a post like that. Or commit to going somewhere that—

Beat.

I'm sorry.

AIDEN: Fine. A sizable donation.

JORDAN: Okay.

AIDEN: And you need to promise me that you're going to tell every sexual partner you have for the next . . . ten years about this.

JORDAN: About . . .

AIDEN: This conversation. That you have an ex who you dated for three years who knows you sexually assaulted her. And you can include your version of things if that makes you feel better. But every sexual partner you have for the next decade needs to have this information so they can make an informed decision about whether they want to be with you.

   Pause.

JORDAN: This isn't—

AIDEN: You just said you wanted to do something.

JORDAN: I know, but this is . . .

AIDEN: Then what do you propose?

   Beat.

JORDAN: I mean . . . If that's really the only . . .

   Silence.

Okay.

AIDEN: Okay?

JORDAN: Okay.

AIDEN: Say, "I promise."

Pause.

JORDAN: I promise.

Beat.

Well, I'm gonna . . .

Beat.

Are you gonna keep . . .

AIDEN: What?

JORDAN: Telling people that I . . .

AIDEN: It's not like I've been . . .

Beat.

I told four people. Close friends. In confidence. I figured Charmagne understood the parameters of that, but apparently not.

JORDAN: Right. I, uh—

JORDAN exhales.

Okay. Okay.

JORDAN moves to go.

AIDEN: One more thing.

JORDAN: What?

AIDEN: I'm going to talk. And you have to listen. You can't say anything. For five minutes. I'm going to set a timer.

JORDAN: Okay.

> *AIDEN gets out her phone and sets a timer. The audience should be able to see it if they try. AIDEN and JORDAN stare at each other. Ten seconds pass.*

Are you—

AIDEN: I'm thinking.

> *Another ten seconds.*

The hardest part was, like
Like, I was . . .
Or, like I had just been

> *Beat.*

Talking about it with people is so . . .
Because you never know what's going to happen
Some people get so angry
Or change the subject
Or burst into tears.

> *Beat.*

That whole summer afterwards, I was just kind of
I watched a lot of TV

I kept the computer in bed with me, and shows would autoplay, so
I'd watch, then fall asleep, then wake up and keep watching.
My dad would send my brothers in to check on me.

   Beat.

I spent a lot of time online,
Which is helpful in theory because it's a distraction
But also the Internet is horrifying.

I've been really into artificial intelligence.
I read somewhere that by the year 2021, there'll be almost as many
personal assistant bots on the planet as people, so everything from
your lighting to your air conditioning to your refrigerator to your
coffee maker could be wired to a system controlled by your voice.

There are a number of ways these devices are designed to make you
feel better.
They don't have faces, which is intentional.
Voices can express certain emotional truths better than faces.
Also, humans seem to have a soft spot for disembodied voices:
God speaking to Adam and Moses,
Your mother's muffled voice while you're still in the womb.

One of the natural next steps after emotion detection will be emotion production,
Like training artificially intelligent agents to be able generate approx-
imations of emotions and do credible performances of, say, empathy,
Eventually turning automated assistants into actual companions.

   Beat.

I don't know.

   Beat.

I tried doing guided meditations for a while,
But I always get distracted thinking about the person recording it.
Did they record in a studio or their laundry room on their phone
while the kids were at soccer?

Beat.

Part of why it's so paralyzing is because no matter what you do, you
always know there's someone somewhere who believes you should
be handling it the exact opposite of the way you're handling it.
If you're angry, especially if you're a woman, especially if you're a
woman of colour, people don't want to see it.
You're expected to hide your feelings, and deal with them in private,
and only come back when you're able to talk about them in a calm,
collected manner. Which means there is literally no time when
you're allowed to actually express your anger or . . .

Beat.

At the same time, if you're not angry enough, some people will
assume you must be lying.
Some people, even people you thought you could count on, will
wonder about your intentions and whether you're just doing this to
ruin someone's reputation.

Pause.

My dad and I were recently driving to the grocery store, listening
to the news. And they were interviewing these women outside a
courthouse, describing the outcome of a trial against their boss,
This very sensitive, articulate, well-educated man.
And as this one woman is describing her experience, my dad says,
"When they get upset like that, it makes it really hard for me to like
them."

Beat.

I'm still not sure what I'm supposed to do with that.

Beat.

This one time my therapist asked "what my grief feels like"
And I was like . . .

Beat.

Because in all honesty, I think you were the one person—
More than anyone else in my life at that time—

AIDEN's phone rings. Five minutes are up.

JORDAN: Was that—

AIDEN: I'm gonna get a glass of water.

Silence while she drinks it.

Well.

Pause.

You should probably . . .

JORDAN: Right.

(*at the door*) Well . . . Thanks for . . . I know this hasn't been an easy
conversation.

Beat.

I . . . Bye, Aiden.

As JORDAN goes to leave—

JORDAN: Sorry, do you know anywhere nearby where I could write / for a few—

AIDEN: I heard you have a book coming out.

JORDAN: Oh. Yeah. Where did you—

AIDEN: Internet.

JORDAN: Right.

AIDEN: You must be . . .

JORDAN: Yeah.

AIDEN: That's great.

JORDAN: Yeah.

AIDEN: Congratulations.

JORDAN: Thanks. Have you been writing at all?

AIDEN: I work a lot.

Pause.

JORDAN: Well, I should—

AIDEN: Who's publishing it?

JORDAN: Oh. Green Moss.

AIDEN: That's exciting.

JORDAN: Yeah.

AIDEN: You don't seem excited.

JORDAN: No, I am. It's just . . .

Beat.

Leonard Cohen used to say it took him ten years to finish a poem. And when I first heard that I was like, okay, buddy. But now that I'm doing the literary equivalent of setting something in stone, I get it. Like, the thought of opening this thing and reading it, and finding mistakes, or ways it could be better makes me feel like—it gives me actual palpitations. Even though it's only a book, right? A book of *poems*. So, who cares? Plus, my editor has a really gentle hand. Like, she keeps saying it's ready, but I'm like, are we looking at the same manuscript here?

AIDEN: I've never met anyone so adept at ruining good news.

JORDAN: No, I'm happy.

Beat.

I'm just also hit time to time by sudden, unexpected, debilitating waves of panic, because I'm trying to get my manuscript as far along as possible before that's it, no more edits, which is hard, because I have no perspective, because I'm so far inside of it, because I've been staring at it every day for the past six months.

Beat.

AIDEN: Are any from back when we were in school?

JORDAN: Oh yeah. A bunch of them are from my thesis project.

AIDEN: (*joking*) Well, I better not be in any of them, otherwise I expect a sizable royalty.

JORDAN: Of course not.

Beat.

I mean you were.

AIDEN: What?

JORDAN: (*quickly*) But I didn't know if you'd be comfortable—so I took them out.

AIDEN: Why would you tell me that?

JORDAN: I thought you were—

AIDEN: I was joking.

JORDAN: I didn't know that.

Beat.

Are you okay?

AIDEN: It's just . . . weird.

JORDAN: I'm sorry.

A weird pause.

AIDEN: Are they . . .

JORDAN: What?

AIDEN: Any good?

JORDAN: I don't know how to answer that.

AIDEN: Like, objectively speaking.

JORDAN: I don't know. I wrote them. I have no objectivity.

AIDEN: I just mean . . . Do you think the collection will suffer without them?

JORDAN: Aiden, it's fine.

AIDEN: I just feel like . . . if they're not—like, if I'm not mentioned by name or anything—

JORDAN: Of course not.

AIDEN: Then I don't really care if you include them.

JORDAN: Really?

Beat.

Because, I mean . . . if you are actually okay with it—I mean, I wouldn't want to include anything you hadn't had the chance to read first, then if you decide they're okay—

AIDEN: As I said, I'm really busy this week, but if you email them to me, I can . . . what? What's wrong?

JORDAN: Nothing.

AIDEN: Then why—

JORDAN: I'm really sorry, but I have to submit my final draft by Monday. And I promised my editor this would be my fourth and final extension.

AIDEN: That's in three days, Jordan, how am I supposed to—

JORDAN: I mean, if you'd be okay with taking a look at them right now—

Pulling out an enormous printed manuscript.

I'm pretty sure there are only three—

AIDEN: Whoa.

JORDAN: What?

AIDEN: Hefty.

JORDAN: I had a lot of free time last year.

AIDEN: *(reading)* Oh my God.

JORDAN: What?

AIDEN: You still do all your edits by hand? How do you send in your draft updates?

JORDAN: You really want to talk about this? I have a printed copy I carry around and rewrite by hand. So, when I have a draft due, I open the last version in Word, then make any edits.

AIDEN: You're going to make all these changes in the next three days?

JORDAN: Typing it up is the easy part. I mean, I won't be sleeping, but it'll get done.

AIDEN: How long have you been working away at this bad boy?

JORDAN: Every morning before work since April. And I took the last two weeks off work so I could hole up in my apartment, making edits for sixteen hours a day. And before that, I spent a week in Victoria, combing through it with Maureen.

AIDEN: *Maureen* agreed to—

JORDAN: In exchange for me helping her landscape her yard this summer.

AIDEN: You went all the way to Victoria for notes you definitely could have gotten over Skype?

JORDAN: It's different.

AIDEN: It's 2019, Jordan. Have you considered integrating a computer into your creative process?

JORDAN: Writing by hand / implicates the body, allowing better access to—

AIDEN: (*teasing*) "Implicates the body, allowing better access to your sense memory."

JORDAN: It's a real thing.

AIDEN: Which ones do you want me to . . .

JORDAN: (*flipping through the manuscript*) This is the first one. It's just those lines at the end.

AIDEN holding up page with a giant "x" across it.

AIDEN: Nice.

JORDAN: I told you I cut it.

AIDEN: "Anxiety." Very upbeat.

She reads it.

It's fine.

JORDAN: Really?

AIDEN: I wouldn't have known if you hadn't told me.

JORDAN: Okay.

Flipping to "Nostalgia."

And this is the second one.

AIDEN reads.

AIDEN: Just those last two stanzas?

JORDAN: Yeah.

AIDEN: Yeah, that's fine.

JORDAN: Great. Okay.

JORDAN flips to the end of the manuscript, then closes it.

And that's it.

AIDEN: I thought you said there were three.

JORDAN: Well, yeah, I mean . . . there was one more. But I'm not going to include it.

AIDEN: Why?

JORDAN: It's not—

AIDEN: It can't be that bad.

JORDAN: No, it's not that, I just—after our conversation, I don't think it's—

AIDEN: Look, Jordan, if this is something you've written about me—

JORDAN: / Yeah, I just don't—

AIDEN: Which multiple people have read, including your editor—

JORDAN: Seriously, I don't think—

AIDEN: Including Maureen—

JORDAN: / It's not like she knew who it—

AIDEN: Then I feel like I have a right to at least—

JORDAN: Okay, okay.

JORDAN hands AIDEN the page with the last poem.

AIDEN: How am I supposed to read this?

JORDAN: What do you mean?

AIDEN: It's got all this—

Holding the page, covered in notes, in front of JORDAN's face.

JORDAN: It's not that bad—

AIDEN: It's a mess. I can't even—

JORDAN: You just have to—

AIDEN handing it to JORDAN.

AIDEN: You read it.

JORDAN: What do you / mean?

AIDEN: Out loud.

JORDAN: Oh. No.

AIDEN: Come on / Jordan.

JORDAN: Please, Aiden, / can we just let it go—

AIDEN: Look, I'm trying do you a fucking favour here, can you just read the fucking poem?

Beat. JORDAN exhales and begins to reluctantly read the poem.

JORDAN: "Eulogy"

Face pressed wet against tile as
You fuck me with a strap-on
in the shower of your apartment.

Had I known this would be the last time
you filled me, would I
have commemorated the occasion?

Said a few words?
Dispatched flowers?
Erected a statue downstairs in the barren courtyard?

Had I paid better attention
Could I have perceived
Your waning attraction,

Dissatisfied cartographer
Mapping the route
Of your eventual departure?

Memory yields only
pounding water, skin, ceramic.
The receptacle

Where you continue to agitate
me, your jostled tree,
yielding fruit.

A weird pause.

Sorry.

AIDEN: Yeah, I'd rather if you didn't—

JORDAN: Of course, that's—why I asked.

A pained silence.

I'm really sorry. I didn't—

AIDEN: It's fine.

Pause.

They're not . . .

JORDAN: What?

AIDEN: Terrible.

JORDAN: You don't have to say that.

AIDEN: I wouldn't if I didn't mean it.

   Beat.

JORDAN: Well, that means a lot coming from you.

AIDEN: Why?

JORDAN: Because you're, like, one of the only people I know who gives actual clear, direct feedback.

AIDEN: You're saying I'm a bitch?

JORDAN: That's the exact opposite of what I'm saying.

   JORDAN's phone chimes. A text message.

Sorry, do you mind if I . . .

AIDEN: Go ahead.

   JORDAN responds to it, then turns the phone to vibrate.
   Meanwhile, AIDEN flips through JORDAN's manuscript.

I forgot your parents sent you to hypnotherapy. And it wouldn't be a Jordan Engles poem if it didn't contain a gratuitous number of references to plant anatomy. "Calyx, corolla, gynoecium." So predictable.

JORDAN: Maybe I can trick people into thinking it's a botany textbook.

AIDEN: Rake in those big botany textbook dollars.

JORDAN: That's the only way I'll make any money off of it.

AIDEN: I thought publishing paid okay.

JORDAN: Oh, it does not. Not unless you're, like, Rupi Kaur.

AIDEN: You just need to add more line breaks.

"The sun
Is shining
Except when
It's not
Lavender
Mother
Beehive
Prayer"

JORDAN: What was I thinking?

AIDEN: I think you might be in this industry for all the wrong reasons. I, for one, am in it for the money.

Beat.

I'm hungry. Are you hungry?

JORDAN: Always. Why?

AIDEN: I tell you what. I'll read your stupid manuscript if you order a pizza.

Beat.

JORDAN: I feel like I should—

AIDEN: Of course.

JORDAN: I appreciate the offer though—

AIDEN: Don't worry about it.

JORDAN: Really.

AIDEN: Have a good night.

JORDAN is about to leave.

JORDAN: I mean . . . I could really use an outside eye.

Beat.

AIDEN: Four cheese. With ranch sauces for dipping. At least, two. No, three. Five.

JORDAN: Deal.

5.

AIDEN addresses the audience.

AIDEN: The town's head scientists held a meeting where they hypothesized how to make the never-ending fires stop. They postulated a correlation between the tides, the earth's greenhouse emissions, and proximity to the sun. However, they had no explanation for the recent and complete lack of rain.

It had been months since the sky opened up, and trees stood in brittle rows, waiting to be watered. The soil ached for moisture. Clouds swelled to gargantuan sizes and rolled heavily over the ground but never burst.

The townspeople petitioned for precipitation in numerous ways. They read articles, conducted experiments, created and signed online petitions, recycled, filmed and aired TV specials featuring prominent local celebrities, made donations to moderately well-researched charities, lambasted their local government officials, bribed holy women, sacrificed high-status goats to deities whose names they could not pronounce, slit their first-borns' throats, slit their second-borns' throats, slit their neighbours' and grandparents' and paramours' throats.

Slowly, people forgot the smell of incoming thunderstorms, the feeling of surprise water droplets cooling their skin. Many children began to forget the meaning of the word "rain" altogether.

After the town's 807th fire, the people took a vote.

6.

> AIDEN's *apartment.* AIDEN *is nearly done* JORDAN's *manuscript. Two empty pizza boxes sit between them.*

AIDEN: I'm not saying you *can't* use second person, it's just whenever anyone does, it feels so—I don't know, bossy. "*You* go upstairs, *you* step outside." My knee-jerk reaction is always, "No, I don't. You don't know me."

JORDAN: Duly noted. Now if you could please try and ignore your deep personal bias throughout the domineering second-person sections—

AIDEN: I never said domineering.

JORDAN: You didn't have to.

> *Beat.*

Do you have anything else to eat?

AIDEN: A full pizza wasn't enough for you?

> JORDAN *gives* AIDEN *a look.*

Check the fridge.

JORDAN does.

JORDAN: Whoa.

JORDAN pulls out an enormous tray of finger foods and carries it over to where AIDEN is sitting.

You still catering for Kelly?

AIDEN: Part-time. Just got a raise, thank you very much. I now make a whopping twenty-two dollars an hour to corral horny eighteen-year-olds. I'm a modern-day chaperone.

(offering one) Try a mushroom cap, they're the best ones.

JORDAN: *(visibly recoiling)* I'm okay.

AIDEN: You still have that weird mushroom / thing?

JORDAN: It's a fungus, it's a literal fungus.

(indicating the platter) So, you just slipped this in your bag when no one was watching?

AIDEN: Technically, our policy is to throw everything out at the end of the night, but I can never bring myself to do it.

JORDAN: Stealing from the rich / to feed the—

AIDEN: Dumpster-diving from the rich. Far less morally objectionable.

AIDEN reads the last few poems. JORDAN picks away at the tray of finger food.

Finished.

JORDAN: And?

AIDEN: I concede: It's not the worst thing I've ever read.

JORDAN: Aiden. Please. Your unbridled enthusiasm is embarrassing.

AIDEN: Okay, okay. It . . . surpasses mediocrity.

JORDAN: I should get you to write the introduction.

Beat.

Have you been sending your stuff out anywhere?

AIDEN: Try everywhere. I feel like I've been rejected by every literary magazine I can think of. I don't even mean major ones—amateur, professional, Canadian, American, doesn't matter. Which I know is part of the job. But then I read the pieces being published over mine, knowing that 76% of the publishing industry is white, and that less than half of what was published last year was written by women, and that less than half of that half was written by women of colour. And I realize the quality of my work only matters so much. What really matters is who I know, and the ways my narrative can serve someone else's agenda. Then I wonder if I was willing to write exclusively about my race or culture in a way that allowed editors to tick a box without taking any actual risks, maybe I'd have a book by now too. Also, where the fuck did Margaret Atwood's ancestors come from?

Beat.

JORDAN: That sounds really frustrating.

AIDEN: Yeah, well.

JORDAN: I mean, if you want—and I totally understand if you don't—I'd be happy to connect you with my editor at Green Moss.

I mean, I can't guarantee it would lead to anything, they get a lot of submissions. But it couldn't hurt.

AIDEN: Uh . . . Wow. I don't know. I mean . . . Maybe. I'll think about it.

Beat.

I wasn't fishing for that, / if that's what you—

JORDAN: No, of course not, I didn't—you're just, like, one of the best writers I know and—

AIDEN: Okay, Jordan—

JORDAN: I mean it. If there's ever any way I can—

The electricity goes out. The apartment is dark except for the light from outside.

AIDEN: Oh for fucking / fuck's sake.

JORDAN: What happened?

AIDEN: My landlord is a giant cheapskate who refuses to fix anything, so the power goes out at least once every couple of months. We've contacted the housing board, but they still haven't done anything about it.

JORDAN: So, what do we . . .

AIDEN: I've got some tealights.

AIDEN goes to the kitchen, using her cellphone as a flashlight. AIDEN turns to JORDAN suddenly.

Sorry, can you . . .

JORDAN: What?

AIDEN: Stand over there.

JORDAN: Why?

AIDEN: Because I can't see anything and I'd feel a lot more comfortable if you were—

JORDAN: Aiden, I'm not going to—

AIDEN: (*distressed*) Can you please just—

JORDAN: (*quickly*) Okay, okay.

> AIDEN *digs around in drawer. Meanwhile,* JORDAN's *phone vibrates. Another text.* JORDAN *types a response. As* AIDEN *returns,* JORDAN *puts the phone away. Using matches,* AIDEN *lights and places tealights around the room.*

How long does it usually take for the power to come back on?

AIDEN: Depends. Sometimes an hour. Sometimes longer. One time after I first moved in, it was out for three days straight.

> JORDAN *watches* AIDEN *light candles.*

JORDAN: And you moved in . . .

AIDEN: Last August.

JORDAN: How's being back in Calgary?

AIDEN: Kind of weird. It's nice to be close to my dad, otherwise I wind up worrying about him all the time. And Taylor's here, so we hang out sometimes. Weather-wise, it's a better fit for me. Not as much rain. Like, I realize now, being back, how much the rain in Victoria was affecting me.

JORDAN: Victoria is nothing compared to Vancouver. Last winter, it rained a hundred days straight.

AIDEN: At least you get flowers in February.

JORDAN: Sometimes.

AIDEN: Most of the time. My grandma's way of punishing us for not visiting more often is texting us pictures of her rhododendrons while we're still waist-deep in snow.

JORDAN: What a sadist.

AIDEN: Total sadist.

AIDEN lights the last tealight.

There.

Beat.

Well, you should probably . . .

JORDAN: Right. Thanks for reading this thing.

AIDEN: Thanks for eating my leftovers before they went rancid.

Silence, except for JORDAN gathering her/his things and heading for the door. It sticks.

JORDAN: Sorry, I still can't—do you think you could—

AIDEN: This whole situation is really fucked, you know that?

AIDEN: (*quickly*) This. Us. Talking like everything's normal.

JORDAN: No, I know, and I'm going, I'm trying to go, I just—

AIDEN: That's what's so fucked up about it: I don't want you to go. What kind of self-destructive bullshit is that? My therapist would have a field day. Yesterday, I was spending my hard-earned money talking about you to a paid professional; today, you're sitting in my apartment, eating pizza and defending your bullshit mushroom phobia, like we're friends again, and it's nice, and I don't know what to do with that—

AIDEN doubles over, clutching her right side.

And now my gallbladder hurts.

JORDAN: Your . . .

AIDEN: (*in pain*) Remember those abdominal pains I used to get all the time?

JORDAN: Yeah . . .

AIDEN: I have gallstones.

JORDAN: Jesus!

AIDEN: They're not life-threatening or anything—they're just these like, little crystallized fat deposits—but if you eat a bunch of greasy shit, like an idiot, you get these fucking gallbladder attacks, and I just ate a whole pizza by myself.

JORDAN: Is there anything I can—

AIDEN: (*needing to sit down*) If it gets really bad, put me in a cab to the ER, and tell the driver to tell a doctor to cut it out of me.

JORDAN: I can't tell if you're serious right now.

AIDEN: It's not a big deal, they cut out my grandma's when she was like, twenty-five, then she lived to be ninety-three, so. Fuck.

JORDAN pulls out a phone and dials.

JORDAN: Can I—do you want me to—

AIDEN: (*continuing to clutch her side*) No, no, no, I just . . .

Pause. It subsides.

Okay. This is what we're going to do. We're going to have a ginger ale, because I want a ginger ale. My gallbladder wants ginger ale. Then you're going to leave. How does that sound to you?

JORDAN: Are you sure?

Beat.

I mean . . . okay.

AIDEN goes to the fridge and gets two ginger ales, handing one to JORDAN.

AIDEN: So, how was Berlin anyway?

JORDAN: Seriously? I didn't go. I thought you knew that.

AIDEN: No.

JORDAN: I spent the summer working at my dad's law firm as an administrative assistant instead. Basically the same thing.

AIDEN: I cannot see you being a good fit for that job.

JORDAN: I was not asked back.

Beat.

How's your dad doing?

AIDEN: Pretty good, I guess. He just retired. It's been kind of a lot. He texts me, like, every five minutes. And he doesn't understand text message etiquette, so his punctuation always makes it seem like he's mad at me.

JORDAN: What do you mean?

AIDEN: He puts periods at the end of everything. So, it's like, "Hello. Period. How are you. Period. Spaghetti. Period. Watching the news. Period." It makes me want to call him and be like, "I'm so sorry, what did I do?"

JORDAN: How're your brothers?

AIDEN: Well, Logan was just grounded for shoplifting, and Max just broke up with his first serious boyfriend, and Jamie got disqualified from the provincial speech and debate tournament. So, it hasn't been an amazing month at the Lee household—a lot of hormones and railing against the injustice of the world—but my dad seems okay. He's just trying to stay optimistic. That's what he says, anyway. "Staying optimistic. Period."

JORDAN: Have you talked to your mom lately?

AIDEN: Not since Christmas. I think she just moved to Mississauga. That's what Logan said, anyway. I think they talked on his birthday.

Beat.

How's Charlie?

JORDAN: She's good. About to start her first year of high school.

AIDEN: Oh my God.

JORDAN: I know. She just got into the school band.

AIDEN: What instrument?

JORDAN: Tuba.

AIDEN: What!

JORDAN: I know. It's amazing. It's, like, three quarters her size. She says she's only doing it for the school trip—

AIDEN: Where?

JORDAN: Winnipeg, I'm pretty sure.

AIDEN: Scenic Winnipeg.

JORDAN: But I think she just really likes the tuba.

AIDEN: How are Benjamin and Margaret?

JORDAN: Oh, you know. Thriving.

AIDEN: They must be happy about the book.

JORDAN: Mmm.

JORDAN gets another text.

AIDEN: Someone's popular.

JORDAN: *(typing a response)* Yeah, right.

AIDEN: What are you doing for work nowadays?

JORDAN: You got your computer handy?

AIDEN hands her laptop to JORDAN. JORDAN opens it.

Heyyy, what's this?

AIDEN, grabbing the laptop back and closing the document:

AIDEN: Nothing.

JORDAN: Looks an awful lot like a story to me.

AIDEN: It's not.

JORDAN: It sure looks like—

AIDEN: Nope. Just a bunch of randomly generated binary code.

JORDAN: So, you are / writing.

AIDEN: Sorry, you're doing what for a living?

JORDAN: Aaaall right. Google "Jameson and Associates."

AIDEN: *(typing)* Oookay . . .

JORDAN: And that is what I do.

AIDEN: You sell houses?

JORDAN: God, no. I manage their website.

AIDEN: And what does that entail?

JORDAN: Taking photos, uploading videos, updating listings . . . I would say "et cetera," but that's literally it.

AIDEN: Wow. That sounds . . .

JORDAN: Mind-numbingly boring. But I get to work from home most of the time, so at very least, I get to be mind-numbingly bored in the comfort of my own apartment.

    Beat.

So?

AIDEN: So?

JORDAN: Whatchaaa writing?

    AIDEN slams her laptop shut and returns it to her desk.

AIDEN: Nothing.

JORDAN: Come on . . .

AIDEN: Just . . . this . . . thing.

JORDAN: Very evocative.

AIDEN: Just a story. About this town. Or fire. Thing. But I'm still trying to figure out how it . . . Anyway.

JORDAN: That's great.

AIDEN: Yeah . . .

Beat.

JORDAN: Guess who I ran into on Granville last month?

AIDEN: Who?

JORDAN: Guess.

AIDEN: Yeah, I'm not going to / do that.

JORDAN: Bilal.

AIDEN: *Bilal!* Oh my God, Bilal. What's he up to now?

JORDAN: He started his own insurance company, which is doing super well. Have you seen his Instagram? It's like, the Eiffel Tower, Machu Pichu, martini, martini, martini.

AIDEN: Is he still writing?

JORDAN: Not at all.

AIDEN: That's so weird! I figured he'd be the first out of everybody to like, be featured on Oprah's Book Club or land a Netflix show or whatever.

JORDAN: I know. Have you seen anyone from school lately?

AIDEN: Taylor, obviously—

JORDAN: How's Taylor?

AIDEN: Pretty good, I think. Writing screenplays and working full-time at an escape room.

JORDAN: Living the dream. Anyone else?

AIDEN: Uh, Spencer, Rae—

JORDAN: What's Rae up to?

AIDEN: Managing a little dance studio on the island.

JORDAN: Nice.

AIDEN: And a couple other people. But—

JORDAN: Like who?

AIDEN: Just some other people in Victoria.

JORDAN: Like . . .

AIDEN: Oh, just, like . . .

Pause.

JORDAN: You mean, like, Charmagne.

AIDEN: And Elise. And Carmen and Joel.

JORDAN: Ah.

Beat.

AIDEN: If it makes you feel any better, Carmen and Joel didn't believe me.

JORDAN: Why would that make me feel better?

Pause.

So, you flew all the way—

AIDEN: Drove.

JORDAN: Drove all the way to Victoria to . . . what?

AIDEN: I wanted to talk about it.

JORDAN: You couldn't at least, I don't know, try contacting me first?

AIDEN: Why?

JORDAN: So we could talk? And you could at least hear my side of things before telling our mutual friend group that I'm some kind of—sexual predator?

AIDEN: I'm allowed to talk to my friends about the significant events of my life.

Beat.

JORDAN: Did it at least . . . I don't know. Help?

AIDEN: Yes. No. I don't know. Elise and I got in a big fight about it.

JORDAN: What do you mean?

AIDEN: She said that by not reporting you or pressing charges, "I'm letting my abuser walk free."

JORDAN: Wow . . . That's . . . Great.

AIDEN: I get where she's coming from. But I also didn't want to be videotaped recounting the details of my sexual assault to a police officer I know doesn't believe me.
Also, I didn't want to have to wait months, if not years, to relive it in front of a jury of strangers.
[ONLY WHEN F JORDAN: Also, in 99% of sexual assaults, the accused perpetrator is male.]
Also, for every one thousand sexual assaults in Canada, three lead to conviction.
[ONLY WHEN F JORDAN: Also, women can't sexually assault other women.]
Also, I'm poor.
Also, your family's loaded.
Also, there are, like, five children's hospitals in five different cities named after your grandfather.
Also, your dad's a lawyer.
Also, you're the nicest, most sincere, well-educated little white [F: girl/M: boy] out there.

> Silence. Eventually, AIDEN gets up and goes over to the fridge and gets a beer.

JORDAN: What are you—

AIDEN: Having a beer. Is that okay?

JORDAN: Oh, I just, uh—

AIDEN: Or are you worried I'm going to get hammered and try to seduce you?

JORDAN: That's not funny.

AIDEN: Who said it was supposed to be funny?

AIDEN opens her beer.

JORDAN: (*standing*) I should probably . . . Deadline.

AIDEN: Right.

JORDAN: You sure you're okay with the . . .?

Indicating the tealights.

AIDEN: Yeah.

As JORDAN is about to leave.

JORDAN: (*simultaneously*) I wasn't trying to—

AIDEN: (*simultaneously*) Look, I don't have—

JORDAN: No, it's not that, I just—

AIDEN: I get it.

Beat.

JORDAN: Have a good night, Aiden.

JORDAN succeeds in getting the door open.

AIDEN: (*blurting*) I got a new crib board. From this garage sale. Or estate sale. I don't know. This guy had just died. Skin cancer or something. That's what his wife said. He collected crib boards. I bought a travel one, which just means it folds up really small. It didn't come with pegs, but we could use matchsticks.

7.

JORDAN's book launch.

JORDAN: This next one is called "Nostalgia."

Beat.

Its origin, late eighteenth century, from Greek:
nostos (return home) and *algos* (pain).
Tampered by grief,

I alphabetize my medicine cabinet,
catalogue inadequacies, cook in the dark,
buy a hunting knife to feel like

anything could happen.
Twelve Rules for Learning A
Language in Three Months.

Free shipping worldwide.
My sister recommends photographing
my genitals.

I weed my mother's garden
and unearth white spoons.
The four main parts of a flower:

calyx, corolla,
androecium, gynoecium.
The worst part of being buried alive

is acceptance. In my dreams,
unassailed by circumstance,
you cut onions in the kitchen

of your old apartment,
open window bathing your hands
and each translucent sliver

in sunlight.

8.

AIDEN's apartment.

Six empty soda cans sit on the coffee table between AIDEN *and* JORDAN. *They play cribbage.*

JORDAN: But there's this guy holding this sign. And I know he's just looking for a reaction. So I try ignoring him. But then he starts yelling at me, and getting up in my face, so, eventually, I can't help it, I start yelling back.

Responding to the look on AIDEN's *face.*

No, I know, believe me, I know.

Beat.

Long story short, he spits in my face—I lose it, we start hitting each other. And there's blood—not a lot of blood, but you know, blood—and police show up, and arrest us, and that should have been the end of it, except I guess a bunch of people filmed it. And uploaded it online. And eventually this family friend sees it and sends it to my mom.

AIDEN: Oh, shit.

JORDAN: I know. And I get this call from my parents where my mom's freaking out at me for putting my safety at risk, meanwhile, my dad's just pissed I'm out protesting. Even though I'm like, "Dad.

It's an anti-fascist rally. Your parents met in a concentration camp."
But he doesn't see it that way. So, we end up in this huge screaming
match where we both say a lot of shit we don't mean and . . . Yeah.
That's what happened.

AIDEN: That's why they cut you off?

JORDAN: Yeah.

AIDEN: When did this all . . .

JORDAN: Uh . . . October, I guess? We haven't really talked since.

    Beat.

I don't know. Things have just been kind of accumulating for a
while.

    Beat.

But it's fine, actually. I feel surprisingly . . . I don't know. It's good.
It's good. Who just dealt?

AIDEN: Me.

JORDAN: Right. Okay. Fifteen–two, four, six, eight, pair is ten.

    Advancing a final peg in the crib board.

And that's game.

AIDEN: Nooooooooooooooo!

JORDAN: Skunked again. I don't know why you like playing so much.
I've literally never seen you win.

AIDEN: I've won.

JORDAN: When?

AIDEN: I don't remember the specific day.

JORDAN's phone rings.

You gonna answer that?

JORDAN: I wasn't planning on it.

AIDEN: Why not?

JORDAN: I'm in the middle of a conversation.

AIDEN: Who wants to get a hold of you so badly?

JORDAN: No one you know.

AIDEN: Try me.

JORDAN: Aiden. There's no way you would know this person.

AIDEN: How do you know?

JORDAN: They live in Vancouver.

AIDEN: I know plenty of people who live in / Vancouver.

JORDAN: And before that they lived in Toronto.

AIDEN: Why are you being so weird about this?

JORDAN: Why are you?

AIDEN: I'm not.

JORDAN: Yes, you are.

AIDEN: Come on
Come on
Come on come on come on
come on come on come on—

JORDAN: Look, it's not—
It's just . . .
My fiancée.

Beat.

AIDEN: Your . . . what?

JORDAN: I'm sorry. I should have told you sooner, but I didn't know how to—

AIDEN: You're getting married?

JORDAN: I wanted to tell you, but I didn't—

AIDEN: I feel like this is the kind of thing that you can just bring up; you don't need to wait for it to come up organically.

JORDAN: I'm sorry—

AIDEN: When?

JORDAN: Next week.

Beat.

AIDEN: Congratulations. Where?

JORDAN: We're just staying in Vancouver.

AIDEN: To who?

JORDAN: You don't know her.

AIDEN: What's her name?

JORDAN: Aiden . . .

AIDEN: What?

JORDAN: I don't think it's a / good idea.

AIDEN: I'm just asking a simple question.

JORDAN: I know that, I just—

AIDEN: And if you don't tell me, then I'll just ask Taylor, or Charmagne, or Elise—

JORDAN: Aiden—

AIDEN: At least one of them has got to have you on social / media.

JORDAN: Fine. Harriet.

AIDEN: What, is she ninety-two? When'd you meet?

JORDAN: Last summer.

AIDEN: So, recently.

JORDAN: Look, I know this is—

AIDEN: Where?

JORDAN: Her parents also have a cabin on Bowen.

AIDEN: Oh, good, so her family's rich too. Thank God. Otherwise, that would've been pretty embarrassing!

JORDAN: Aiden—

AIDEN: Where'd you pop / the question?

JORDAN: I'm sorry, I can see I've upset you—

AIDEN: Why would I be upset? I'm happy! Why shouldn't I be happy for my friend on the brink of domestic bliss?

JORDAN: Then do you think you could maybe lower your voice?

AIDEN: Does she know about me?

JORDAN: What do / you mean?

AIDEN: Does she know you're here?

JORDAN: No, I—

AIDEN: Because you're going to have to—I mean, you promised you would tell all of your—

JORDAN: I know. And I will.

AIDEN: Good.

JORDAN: I'm really sorry, I obviously shouldn't have mentioned it—

AIDEN: I assume my invitation is still in / the mail?

JORDAN: Is there any way we can—

AIDEN: Why are you telling me this?

JORDAN: I thought you would want to know.

AIDEN: Why? Why would you think that?

JORDAN: I don't know, I just—

AIDEN: We hadn't spoken in TWO YEARS.

JORDAN: I know—

AIDEN: TWO YEARS, Jordan.

JORDAN: I know!

AIDEN: You know why? Because I don't want to know about you, or your life! I don't want to have anything to do with you!

Beat.

I haven't been with anyone else since you. I've tried. But the idea of someone . . .

Beat.

Meanwhile, you—you have a fiancée! We should celebrate.

JORDAN: Aiden—

AIDEN: We should have a toast. **JORDAN:** No, I should go, I'm
Come on, let's have a toast! sorry for—

AIDEN: I WANT TO GIVE A TOAST, LET ME GIVE A TOAST.

JORDAN: Okay. Okay. We'll have a toast.

AIDEN goes to the fridge, gets them both a soda water, then creates a "microphone" out of something in the apartment.

AIDEN: *(raising her can)* Thank you, everyone, for taking the time out of your busy schedules to be here to celebrate with us here today. It means a lot. To Jordan and Agatha—

JORDAN: Harriet—

AIDEN: I haven't known the two of you long
As a couple, per se
But I really couldn't be more delighted
So, let's all raise a glass—
Raise your glass, Jordan—
Let's all raise a glass—
To my dear friend Jordan Engels
As we implore the heavens to smile down on upon this most blesséd of unions
Forever and ever
Amen

JORDAN: Are you done?

Silence.

Aiden, it's not like—

AIDEN: What?

Beat.

JORDAN: Nothing. I should go.

JORDAN collects her/his things. Beat.

I'm sorry. I was just trying to . . .

AIDEN: No. It's good, actually. This is good.

Beat.

AIDEN: Well, you should—   **JORDAN:** Hey, is there any chance you're still—

AIDEN: What?

JORDAN: *(quickly)* Nothing. Sorry.

AIDEN: What, Jordan?

JORDAN: I, uh . . . I was going to ask if you were still . . . uh . . .

AIDEN: Spit it out.

JORDAN: Hair. Cutting.

AIDEN: Sorry?

JORDAN: Just—I was going to see if you'd be open to—cutting my . . .

AIDEN: Seriously?

JORDAN: It was a stupid idea, I'm just gonna—

AIDEN: You don't have a hairdresser in Vancouver?

JORDAN: I do, she just always cuts it way too short.

AIDEN: Why don't you go somewhere else?

JORDAN: Because she's a friend of a friend, and we see each other at parties all the time, so if I start going somewhere else, it'll be this whole—

AIDEN: You're unbelievable.

Beat.

You'd have to pay me.

JORDAN: (*searching pockets*) I can give you . . . eighteen dollars . . . and . . . a Starbucks gift card.

AIDEN: How much is on it?

JORDAN: Twenty bucks. Or it used to be twenty bucks. Actually, I have no idea.

Beat.

AIDEN: . . . Fine.

AIDEN goes to the kitchen, then returns with a hair-cutting smock. She puts it around JORDAN's neck. AIDEN takes off JORDAN's glasses and hands them to him/her.

(*brandishing scissors*) Do you have any idea how easy it would be for me to slit your throat right now?

JORDAN: Aiden . . .

AIDEN: (*lightening*) Relax! I'm just kidding. God.

She commences cutting JORDAN's hair. Beat.

So, what kind of ceremony are you having?

JORDAN: You don't have to—

AIDEN: It's fine.

Beat.

JORDAN: We're just keeping things really simple. We're not having any formal—

AIDEN: Melon-caprese-skewers simple or city hall simple?

JORDAN: I don't know how to answer that.

AIDEN: I feel like it's pretty—

JORDAN: City hall simple, but only because—

AIDEN: What? But you always wanted a whole—

JORDAN: People change.

AIDEN: And your parents are okay with that?

JORDAN: They're not coming.

AIDEN: What?

JORDAN: I told you, we're not . . .

AIDEN: What about Charlie?

JORDAN: What about her?

AIDEN: Is she going?

JORDAN: Yes.

Beat.

I mean, I invited her. She still hasn't RSVPed.

AIDEN: Oh fuck.

JORDAN: What?

AIDEN: "Oh fuck" in the good way.

JORDAN: What'd you do?

AIDEN: Nothing.

JORDAN: Seriously—

AIDEN: If you weren't looking for it, you'd never notice.

JORDAN: (*trying to get up*) Maybe this wasn't such a / good idea.

AIDEN: Look, I know what I'm doing. My aunt is a hairdresser, remember?

JORDAN: Your aunt got sued for cutting off part of a guy's—

AIDEN: (*shushing*) Ah-pah-buh-buh-buh. I got this.

   She keeps cutting.

Does Hattie—

JORDAN: / Harriet—

AIDEN: Let you have sleep sex?

JORDAN: We are not discussing this.

AIDEN: What? I'm just—

JORDAN: No.

AIDEN: Fine.

Beat.

Prude.

She keeps cutting.

9.

JORDAN's book launch.

JORDAN: This is my last one.

Beat.

I used to end this collection with another poem, but I . . . changed it. So, the one you're about to hear is brand new. If you hate it, please don't tell me, 'cause the book's printed, and there's nothing I can do about it now. Thanks again for being such a great audience.

Beat.

"Awakening"

Beat.

Do we understand each other better now?
A controlled burn is defined as a wildfire
intentionally set for a variety of reasons:
Prairie restoration, farming,
regeneration, regrowth, renewal.
Cones from lodgepole pines and sequoias
require heat from fire to open and disperse their seeds.

I arrive home.
She waits on the couch in the dark
and asks all the questions one asks:
Where were you? What happened? Whose clothes?
The absence of an answer
Is still an answer.

Parting is the point when two people separate
Or a decision is made.

What I've learned:
How to be left again.
The sparseness of an empty bed.
Guilt is irrelevant.
Intention is irrelevant.
Memory dangles alternate realities like a lure but is ultimately irrelevant.

Do we understand each other better now?

10.

Present. AIDEN's *apartment. She holds up a mirror.*

JORDAN: You've gotten way better.

AIDEN: I've been practising. On myself, but still.

Sweeping up the cut hair.

And just think, for years to come, the hundreds of rodents inhabiting this apartment building will be insulating their homes with your hair. It's humbling.

JORDAN: It's horrifying.

AIDEN pulls a joint out of a hollowed-out book in her bookshelf.

What book?

AIDEN: *(lighting the joint)* The Book of Martyrdom and Artifice.

JORDAN: Ginsberg.

AIDEN: I feel like he'd be into it.

AIDEN takes a toke, and then tries to pass it to JORDAN.

So, what are you—

JORDAN: I'm good, actually.

AIDEN: What?

JORDAN: I'm not really smoking weed right now.

AIDEN: You're kidding.

JORDAN: Or doing any drugs, actually.

AIDEN: Really?

JORDAN: Oh, I just like . . . After graduating, I was kind of a mess. And I was spending all my free time with these friends from high school who partied a lot and working this job I hated. Then one night, during Charlie's sixteenth birthday party—a pool party, very fun—one of her friends found me in the family changeroom after doing a bunch of cocaine and I made her call an ambulance because I was convinced I was having a heart attack.

Beat.

Plus, there's the whole fentanyl . . . I don't really miss it.

AIDEN: Do you want me to . . .?

Indicates putting the joint out.

JORDAN: Oh no, it's fine. I don't mind.

AIDEN: I feel kind of weird about—

JORDAN: It's not a big deal.

AIDEN: I'm just gonna . . .

She puts it out.

Pause.

JORDAN: Well, I should . . . Thanks for the haircut.

AIDEN: Couldn't have you getting hitched looking like a ragamuffin.

Beat.

Happy wedding . . . thing.

JORDAN: Thanks.

AIDEN: I've never been one for matrimonial . . . anything . . .

JORDAN: Really? I hadn't noticed.

AIDEN: But I hope yours is one of the good ones.

JORDAN: Thanks.

AIDEN: And who knows, if it's not under water by then, maybe you and Harriet can retire to sunny Alaska.

JORDAN: How did you know that?

AIDEN: Know what?

JORDAN: That Harry's family is from Alaska.

AIDEN: What? I didn't. I just—

JORDAN: How did you know that? Did Charmagne tell you that, or Taylor, or Elise, or—

AIDEN: Nobody told me, okay, / now can you—

JORDAN: Then how did you know that, Aiden?

AIDEN: Can you back off, please, / you're making me—

JORDAN: It's not a big deal, but I need you to tell me how you / knew that.

AIDEN: I saw it on your fucking Facebook profile, okay?

JORDAN: You deleted me off Facebook.

AIDEN: I was at Taylor's, and they left their laptop open, and I looked at your profile for, like, five seconds, I don't see what the big deal is.

JORDAN: You just acted like I was a giant fucking asshole for not telling you about Harry right away, and the whole time you knew I was engaged?

AIDEN: I didn't know you were engaged!

JORDAN: Why?

AIDEN: Why what?

JORDAN: Why did you do that?

AIDEN: I don't see what—

JORDAN: Why were you looking me up on social media?

AIDEN: Because I like to know where my abuser is and what [**F:** she's / **M:** he's] doing, I don't see what's so mind-blowing about that.

JORDAN: Really?

AIDEN: Yes, really!

JORDAN: And when you asked me to promise that I was going to tell all my future partners about this thing, you knew that I—

AIDEN: I knew that you were dating a woman who had no idea you had sexually assaulted your last partner! Then I spent the month after debating whether to message her, because I felt like I had a responsibility, like, even if I don't know this woman, I have a responsibility, because I think the people you're fucking have a right to know this thing, don't you?

Pause.

JORDAN: I'm sorry. I didn't . . . I'm going to tell her. I promised I'd tell her and I'm going to tell her.

Pause.

AIDEN: You should go.

JORDAN: Yeah.

Pause.

I . . . Sorry again about this whole . . . And how everything . . . I'm just . . . really sorry.

As JORDAN is at the door.

AIDEN: On your way out, make sure / that you—

What?

What the fuck did you just say?

Answer the fucking question, Jordan—

JORDAN: I'm still in love with you.

I'm sorry—

I shouldn't have said that, I'm gonna—

I'm sorry, that was a really fucked up thing to say.

AIDEN: What the fuck, man! What the fuck am I supposed to say to that?

JORDAN: I know—

AIDEN: Like, do you have any idea—after everything I told you—

JORDAN: No, I know, I just needed you to know, / before I—

AIDEN: What the actual fuck is wrong with you! You're engaged! To another woman! Who I don't know much about, but I'm betting doesn't deserve—

JORDAN: I know, I just—

AIDEN: And even if you weren't, there is no way I would ever—

JORDAN: I know—

AIDEN: Not if you were the last fucking—

JORDAN: No, I know that, I just—

AIDEN: And the fact you would show up here and tell me that is yet another indication your needs will always come before everyone else's—

JORDAN: Believe me, I'm not trying to—it's not like I thought you would—but I couldn't just—you're right, you're right, you're right—

JORDAN: (*with momentum*) She doesn't deserve this, and neither do you, it's totally fucked that I'm still here, but the thought of—I think of you every day, Aiden. Every single fucking day. Before I met you, I thought I'd never—even as a kid, I always felt like—I'd just kind of made peace with the fact I was never going to meet anyone I could be my whole self with. I don't even mean romantically; I mean literally anyone. And ever since we—I haven't—you are the only person on the planet I know how to have a conversation with. I hate everyone else. I don't hate them. They're just not—no one jokes, or writes, or listens, or laughs, or asks questions, or calls me on my shit like you. And the thought of going the rest of my life without telling you, without at least trying to fight for, I don't know, us—

AIDEN: There is no us!

JORDAN: Then why am I still here?

AIDEN: I don't know, because—

JORDAN: Because every time I try to leave, we keep coming up with—

AIDEN: Jordan, I can't, I'm sorry. You broke it.

JORDAN: There must be something I can do.

AIDEN: Tell me you admit it, and you take responsibility, and you're going to get help so you can understand why you did what you did.

JORDAN: I wish I could, but I—

AIDEN: Why not?

JORDAN: Because I didn't—

AIDEN: You did.

JORDAN: I'm sorry, Aiden, I know that I didn't, so I can't—

AIDEN: Then I can't—

JORDAN: Is there anything else I can—you don't need to answer right away, you can take some time to think about it.

AIDEN: I told you, but if you can't—

JORDAN: What if we started over?

AIDEN: How, Jordan? How are we supposed to do that?

JORDAN: We could take it really slowly. My name is Jordan Engels, nice to / meet you.

AIDEN: That's not how it works.

JORDAN: You don't even want to try?

AIDEN: I'm sorry, Jordan.

JORDAN: Please.

AIDEN: You're just making this—

JORDAN: You're saying there's no part of you that misses—

AIDEN: It's not—I just—

AIDEN grabs and kisses JORDAN suddenly. She releases him/her just as quickly, horrified with herself.

JORDAN and AIDEN stare at one another.

JORDAN and AIDEN kiss. They make out. It is familiar, heated, and uncertain. They figure it out as they go.

There is only one tealight left—all the rest have gone out.

JORDAN pulls away.

Pause.

JORDAN: What are you thinking?

Very slowly, AIDEN brings JORDAN onto the bed. They continue to make out, with AIDEN guiding. It escalates. Eventually, one of JORDAN's hands moves toward AIDEN's belt. AIDEN grabs and pins JORDAN's hands above his/her head.

Their clothes come off, one by one.

By the end of this, JORDAN is fully naked. AIDEN's bra may come off, but her bottom underwear stays on.

They lie down together in bed and keep kissing.

11.

AIDEN addresses the audience.

AIDEN: A philosophical question (entertained by the town's greatest thinkers): What do you do when your entire life is on fire? What do you do when every morning, you wake up to the taste of ash, blissfully unaware of its source, before remembering and experiencing the sinking feeling?

The reality is every object you have ever treasured is on fire. Every bed you have ever slept in has been reduced to cinders. All the pets you couldn't smuggle into your bag or under your arm or inside your pockets are unambiguously ash.

Eventually, you begin to wonder, why fight it? A local magazine offers some fun ways to yield to it: Roll yourself in sawdust. Wash your hair in gasoline. Exfoliate with ether. It's only a tragedy if you don't want it to happen.

The town's citizens meet at city hall and take off all their clothes. They stack piles of wood, which reach higher than the ghost of the town's tallest skyscraper. They light a match. They light thousands of matches. They inhale. They breathe the black smoke and cough. It's okay. It's a relief. It is. The flames rise. The citizens hold their loved ones and prepare to be extinguished, snuffed out completely in a matter of minutes.

Then something happens: something only the oldest citizens remember happening in their lifetimes.

From the part of the sky where cloud meets smoke: it begins to snow.

AIDEN blows out the last tealight.

12.

Early morning.

AIDEN and JORDAN lay intertwined in bed. AIDEN is awake. She hasn't slept. She stares out.

AIDEN is overcome by nausea. She silently extracts herself from JORDAN, then goes over to the sink and gags. Nothing comes up. It passes.

AIDEN stares at JORDAN for a while, then makes a decision. She puts on clothes and prepares to leave. When she is at the door, she turns back and looks at JORDAN's sleeping body.

Pause.

AIDEN sees JORDAN's manuscript, goes over to it, then pulls out and re-reads the last poem: "Eulogy." AIDEN searches for the matches she used on the candles, then retrieves a metal garbage can. She fills it with stray paper, then strikes a match, then lights "Eulogy" on fire, placing it in the garbage. AIDEN drops JORDAN's credit cards, wallet, cellphone, and clothes inside as well. The fire builds.

AIDEN picks up JORDAN's manuscript again and flips through it.

The fire alarm goes off. JORDAN wakes up.

JORDAN: *(seeing the fire)* What—

Seeing the manuscript in AIDEN's hands.

Wait—

Without breaking eye contact, AIDEN drops a small section of the manuscript into the fire. JORDAN runs to rescue it but is too late. They both stare into the can and watch the pages burn.

AIDEN holds the rest of the manuscript over the fire. AIDEN and JORDAN look at each other. Silence.

JORDAN takes a step away from the fire, yielding.

They continue to stare at one another. AIDEN drops the rest of the manuscript inside.

The fire rises high in the metal container.

AIDEN is still. JORDAN is still.

The electric sprinklers come to life. They look up. Rain.

Eventually, AIDEN and JORDAN are drenched.

AIDEN picks up her bag, keys, and jacket. Before exiting, she turns back.

AIDEN: Goodbye, Jordan.

AIDEN leaves the apartment. JORDAN is left alone, naked. JORDAN looks inside the garbage can, taking stock of the damage and searching for clothes. AIDEN speaks to the audience over top.

On the day later referred to by historians as The Day That Changed Everything, the townspeople watched, stunned, naked, as the icy flakes descended fast and wet and thick as eyelashes. One citizen recalls feeling like she had woken up from a month-long fever. Another said it was like finding your keys years after losing them in a breadbox, in a guesthouse, in a foreign country.

Something in the townspeople stirred. And despite history, despite logic, they filled buckets, washbasins, pitchers, and casserole dishes with water, then launched them one by one like waves onto the inferno. After years of burns and heat exhaustion, the townspeople listened as the last ember released its last hiss, and the seemingly insatiable fire went out. The townspeople waited, convinced another would take its place. But days went by without incident. Then weeks. Months. Dizzy with hope, hardly daring to believe their luck, the townspeople began to rebuild.

JORDAN leaves the apartment.

A fire's effects may continue to be felt long after it's been put out. This is evidenced by the fact that every so often, some well-meaning citizen mistakes a wisp of cloud for a column of smoke and sounds the alarm, causing the other townspeople to stop what they're doing as memory opens inside them like a penknife. The heat, suffocating; the smell, nauseating; the sounds, muffled at first then inexplicably loud; the animal body in crisis.

Visualizations help. Water helps. Remember, every moment, good or bad, will inevitably be replaced by another moment.

Eventually, the townspeople realize their mistake and go back to whatever it was they were doing before the interruption: hanging laundry, buying lightbulbs, microwaving leftovers. The sacred and mundane tasks that create the illusion, then reality, of normalcy and assert the possibility of life after fire.

Sound of rain builds. Lights fade.

End of play.

ABOUT THE CONTRIBUTORS

Elena (or Eli) **Belyea** (they/she) is a queer playwright, performer, producer, and arts educator from Amiskwaciwâskahikan (colonially known as Edmonton) on Treaty 6 territory. They're also the artistic director of Tiny Bear Jaws, an agile femme- and queer-run independent theatre company. Her plays have been produced internationally. Elena is also half of queer sketch duo Gender? I Hardly Know Them (@genderihardlyknowthem). More at elenabelyea.com.

Thea Fitz-James (she/her) is part academic and part theatre practitioner. She holds a PH.D. in Performance Studies at York University, where she wrote about queer performances of textiles in activism and performance art. Thea is a theatre-maker and performance artist, having created work with FADO Performance Art Centre in Toronto (*Daughter's Disease*), Secret Theatre in Halifax (*No Filter*), SummerWorks (*Naked Ladies*), and the School of Making Thinking in New York. Her solo performance piece, *Naked Ladies*, made international news when it was banned in Singapore in 2017, and her other solo show, *Drunk Girl*, has toured internationally to the US and Australia. She has curated performance festivals for the Cucalorus Festival and has taught courses in theatre history and theatre for social justice. Thea was key in initiating the consent movement on the Canadian fringe circuit, co-authoring and disseminating a letter to the fringe festivals signed by two hundred-fifty fringe artists. She is currently working as a program manager for Artscape Toronto, managing their project artsUNITE. Thea Fitz-James identifies as part of the queer community (as a pan/bisexual), and part of the "Mad" community, as manic, and is a white, cis female settler.

Frances Koncan (she/they) was born many years ago and is now of a certain age. Originally from Couchiching First Nation in Treaty 3 territory, she currently lives and works in Winnipeg, Manitoba, in Treaty 1 territory. She is a writer, director, a Taurus, an INFP, an Enneagram Type 4, and mother to a dog named Tucker, a cat named Tucker, and fifty-eight houseplants who are not named Tucker. A graduate of CUNY Brooklyn College's M.F.A. playwriting program, her career began in 2015 and has been on a very slow but modestly upward trajectory ever since. Her greatest dream is to write a Hallmark movie.

Lindsay Lachance (Algonquin Anishinaabe) has worked as a dramaturg for over a decade and has a PH.D. from the Department of Theatre and Film at the University of British Columbia. Lindsay's dramaturgical practice is influenced by her relationship with birch bark biting and the Gatineau River. She is also the director of the Animikiig Creators Unit at Native Earth Performing Arts, which focuses on the development of new Indigenous works.

Michelle MacArthur is Assistant Professor at the University of Windsor's School of Dramatic Art. Her research focuses on four main, intersecting areas: equity in theatre, theatre criticism, contemporary Canadian theatre, and feminism and performance. Her work has appeared in several edited collections and journals including *Theatre Research in Canada*, *Canadian Theatre Review*, and *Contemporary Theatre Review*. As an editor, she has edited the periodical *alt.theatre: cultural diversity and the stage* (2016–18) and co-edited two issues of *Canadian Theatre Review* as well as the book *Performing Adaptations: Essays and Conversations on the Theory and Practice of Adaptation* (Cambridge Scholars Publishing, 2009). With support from the Social Sciences and Humanities Research Council of Canada, she is currently working on multiple projects about the changing state of theatre criticism in Canada. She is a millennial by most definitions.

Jenna Rodgers (she/her) is a mixed-race director and dramaturg who gratefully resides on land called Moh'kins'tsis (Calgary), on Treaty 7 Territory. She is the founding artistic director of Chromatic Theatre—a company dedicated to producing and developing work by and for racialized artists. Jenna is also the dramaturg for the Playwrights Lab at the Banff Centre for Arts and Creativity, the board co-chair of the Literary Managers and Dramaturgs of the Americas, and the Artstrek director for Theatre Alberta. She is a passionate arts equity advocate, a graduate of the National Theatre School's Artistic Leadership Residency (2020), the Banff Centre's Cultural Leadership program (2019), and a member of the artEquity National Facilitator Training cohort (2018). She was shortlisted for the 2021 Gina's Prize and is a recipient of a 2018 Lieutenant Governor of Alberta Emerging Artist Award. She holds an M.A. in International Performance Research from the universities of Amsterdam and Tampere.

Erin Shields is a Montreal-based playwright. Erin's adaptation of *Paradise Lost* premiered at the Stratford Festival and won the Quebec Writers' Federation Playwriting Prize. Erin won the 2011 Governor General's Literary Award for Drama for her play *If We Were Birds*, which premiered at Tarragon Theatre. Other theatre credits include: *Piaf/ Dietrich* (Mirvish Productions/Segal Centre), *The Lady from the Sea* (Shaw Festival), *The Millennial Malcontent* and *Soliciting Temptation* (Tarragon Theatre), and *Instant* (Geordie Theatre). Upcoming projects include *Queen Goneril* for Soulpepper, *Jane Eyre* for the Citadel Theatre, and *Ransacking Troy* for the Stratford Festival.

Kailin Wright is Associate Professor and Jules Léger Research Scholar in the Humanities and Social Sciences at St. Francis Xavier University. Her monograph, *Political Adaptation in Canadian Theatre*, was published by McGill-Queen's University Press in 2020. Kailin has also published a critical edition of Carroll Aikins's *The God of Gods: A Canadian Play* (University of Ottawa Press, 2016) and articles in *Theatre Journal*, *Canadian Literature*, *Studies in Canadian Literature*, *Canadian Theatre Review*, and *Theatre Research in Canada*. Winner of the Association of Atlantic Universities (AAU) Distinguished Teaching Award (2021), her research and teaching focuses on adaptation, feminist performance, theatre history, motherhood, futurity, and race in Canadian theatre. Kailin holds a federal Social Sciences and Humanities Research Council of Canada grant for her current book project, *No Baby, No Future: Performing Motherhood and Loss*.